Stoicism & Empathy

A Perfectly Balanced Match for Boosting Mental Toughness, Analyzing People, and Strengthening Emotional Intelligence. A Beginner's Guide to the Empathic and Stoic Way of Life

Daniel Brown

© Copyright 2020 by Daniel Brown. All right reserved.

The work contained herein has been produced with the intent to provide relevant knowledge and information on the topic on the topic described in the title for entertainment purposes only. While the author has gone to every extent to furnish up to date and true information, no claims can be made as to its accuracy or validity as the author has made no claims to be an expert on this topic. Notwithstanding, the reader is asked to do their own research and consult any subject matter experts they deem necessary to ensure the quality and accuracy of the material presented herein.

This statement is legally binding as deemed by the Committee of Publishers Association and the American Bar Association for the territory of the United States. Other jurisdictions may apply their own legal statutes. Any reproduction, transmission, or copying of this material contained in this work without the express written consent of the copyright holder shall be deemed as a copyright violation as per the current legislation in force on the date of publishing and subsequent time thereafter. All additional works derived from this material may be claimed by the holder of this copyright.

The data, depictions, events, descriptions, and all other information forthwith are considered to be true, fair, and accurate unless the work is expressly described as a work of fiction. Regardless of the nature of this work, the Publisher is exempt from any responsibility of actions taken by the reader in conjunction with this work. The Publisher acknowledges that the reader acts of their own accord and releases the author and Publisher of any responsibility for the observance of tips, advice, counsel, strategies, and techniques that may be offered in this volume.

Table of Contents

Introduction 1
Chapter 1: Stoicism Vs. the Empath 4

   The Purpose of Emotions and Empathy 4
   Rationality Vs. Emotionality.. *12*
   Introducing the Empath *13*
   Introducing Stoicism.. *16*
   Who Is the Stoic Empath?... *18*

Chapter 2: Understanding the Empath 21

   Empaths Absorb Emotions *22*
   Empaths Struggle in Public *24*
   Empaths Feel the Energy in the Room *25*
   Empaths Understand the Perspectives of Others *26*
   Empaths Attract People in Need of Help.............................*27*
   Empaths Struggle With Difficult News *28*
   Empaths Love Pets and Babies..*29*
   Empaths Struggle With Emotional Contagion *29*
   Empaths Struggle in Relationships......................................*30*
   Empaths Are Easy Targets for Abuse *31*
   Empaths Need Time Alone..*32*

Chapter 3: Pros and Cons of the Empath's Power ... 33

   Pros to Being an Empath *34*
   Cons to Being an Empath *38*

Chapter 4: Protecting the Empathic Self................. 45

   Shielding Visualization *46*
   Expressing Your Needs *47*
   Setting Boundaries...*49*
   Preventing Overload..*50*
   The Empathic Protector Meditation.................................... *51*

Journal Regularly *53*
Avoid Toxic People *54*

Chapter 5: Finding Peace and Happiness as an Empath 56

Spend Time Alone *57*
Spend Time in Nature *58*
Have Meaningful Conversations *59*
Spare Yourself From Negative People *60*
Have Partners Who Are Supportive *61*
Practice Mindfulness *62*
Acceptance *63*
Hobbies *65*
Self-Compassion *66*

Chapter 6: Virtues in Stoicism 67

A Closer Look at Stoicism *68*
The Virtues *70*

Chapter 7: The Stoic Life Is the Good Life 79

Control the Thinking *80*
Train the Mind *83*
Practice Acceptance *84*
Practice Minimalism *86*
Practice Gratitude *87*
Be Kind and Cheerful *88*
Practice What You Preach *89*

Chapter 8: Stoicism and Emotions 92

The Stoics and Joy Versus Pleasure *95*
The Stoics and Wish Versus Lust *97*
The Stoics and Caution Versus Fear *99*

Chapter 9: Finding Inner Peace 103

Let Go of Anxiety *105*

Accept Mortality..*106*
Remember Whose Opinions Matter the Most..................*108*
Take Time to Be Still *110*
Find the Beauty in Every Situation *111*
Imagine a New Perspective *112*
Follow Your Code *113*
Reflect *114*

Chapter 10: Tips and Strategies on Finding the Right Balance Between Stoicism and Empathic Ways of Life... 116

Develop Your Control...*118*
Protect Your Time *119*
Recognize Happiness Is From Within..............................*119*
Keep Your Focus..*120*
Get Rid of Ego..*121*
Write Often *122*
Be Firm *122*
Imagine the Worst Case Scenario *123*
Accept That Nothing Lasts Forever...................................*124*

Conclusion **126**

Introduction

Stop and think about the word stoicism for a moment—most people immediately conjure up the image of someone standing, blank faced and unmoving, physically and emotionally. It is easy to get caught up in the word's meaning, which, according to the dictionary, is:

Stoic: A person who can endure pain or hardship without showing their feelings or complaining.

All too often, however, people misunderstand that definition. Instead of not showing feelings or complaints, many people instead jump to the conclusion that if there are no emotions on the surface, then there are probably no emotions under the surface either. They assume that to be stoic, you must be cruel, or at the very least, emotionally shut off and blank. What they are missing, however, is that you can be outwardly blank, hiding the pains or struggles that you are suffering through, while internally still having all sorts of emotions. Just because you do not show your emotions outwardly does not mean that they are not there—it just means that you are in control of them.

Likewise, people tend to misunderstand what it means to be empathic. They assume that the empath is some emotionally volatile wreck who cannot walk into a crowded room without melting down at all of the emotions around them that they are sensing. This, too, is a bit of a misconception. You can be empathic, but also in control of your emotions as well. Both empaths and stoics share one thing in common: You are working to better yourself. Contrary to popular belief, you can be stoic and empathic at the same time—there is no real dichotomy between the two. They can be one and the same without a problem—you just have to be willing to work to allow both to be present at the same time.

Within this book, we are going to be addressing both stoicism and becoming an empathic individual. You can do both if you know what you are doing and you are willing to put in the effort. As you read through this book, you will discover that you can not only tap into your ability to understand other people, but also to allow yourself to be unburdened of the control of your emotions.

Ultimately, emotions are very important, and they hold a special power over us—they control us and influence what it is that we do and how we interact with the world. They are there to instinctively guide you through life so that you can stay alive. We evolved them for a reason—and that reason was for instincts.

As you read through this book, you will first be introduced to the idea of the empath, and from there, you will start to understand the stoic as well. The idea that you will be working toward is that it is possible to live a life that will embrace both concepts, recognizing that there is, in fact, a way to balance out stoicism with empathic life values to discover the perfect way to approach the world. If you can do that, you will find that you will be able to enjoy life much more. You will be able to reject the idea of dichotomies; you can be stoically empathic, or empathically stoic, and you will actually see that being able to innately and deeply understand humankind around you while also being able to restrain yourself from being controlled by those feelings is actually a highly beneficial way to get through life. If you can balance out stoicism with empathy, you get the best of both worlds all at once—you are able to live virtuously.

Chapter 1: Stoicism Vs. the Empath

To begin, we have to stop and look at both the empath and the stoic. Upon understanding both of them, we can begin to paint a picture of the stoic empath, someone who is able to feel deeply without becoming frenzied or passionate. It is someone who is able to retain control over themselves, even when things seem bleak or frustrating. As we read through this chapter, we will be going over the basic understanding of what the principles of stoicism are, what the idea behind an empath is, and what happens when you combine the two together.

The Purpose of Emotions and Empathy

Emotions and empathy are important—so important that we have them deeply ingrained into us. We have specifically evolved to have both emotions and empathy, as evidenced in the brain. We have areas in the brain that are specific to various emotions, and structures within the brain that are specific to regulating them. The amygdala, for example, a small structure deep in the brain, is responsible for the integration of emotions, behavior, and motivation. Empathy is equally important to the evolution of humanity—we are naturally empathetic to the point that we have mirror neurons—neurons throughout the brain that activate when you see someone else doing something. For example, if you see someone else laughing, the area in your brain that controls laughter activates—but only the mirror neurons. You can understand the emotions and actions of others through these empathetic motor neurons—but why do we have them? Are they really as important as they seem?

Defining emotions

Emotions, then, are the feelings that we have—they are motivators. Emotions have three distinct parts to them:

- **The subjective component:** This is how you experience the emotion that you are having

- **The physiological component:** This is the response that your body has to the emotion that you are having

- **The expressive component:** This is the behavioral response that you have to your emotions

Each of these elements plays a part in the idea of an emotion, motivating us into action. They are there specifically for that point. Think about the last time you watched an animal walking around—they clearly feel emotions to some degree.

Dogs, for example, can very clearly feel happiness, sadness, guilt, anger, and fear without a problem. We know this. We can tell when they are happy and sad. They have these emotions because they drive behaviors that are evolutionarily valuable. We feel fear to avoid something to keep ourselves alive. We get angry to protect ourselves from a perceived threat. We are happy to reinforce a behavior again. We are simple creatures at heart—our emotions are there to guide us if we let them.

However, emotions are not all-powerful. Notice how they are listed as motivational, but not as controlling. Emotions cannot control you unless you surrender yourself to them, known as letting yourself be led by passions. Passions, according to stoicism, should not be able to control you. We will be going over these in depth later in the book.

Emotions are only as powerful as you allow them to be—if you allow them to lead your behavior, they will. However, you can also learn to overcome them completely; you can discover what you can do to prevent yourself from being led by them. This is the entire premise behind stoicism—you do not let yourself be ruled by emotions.

The seven universal emotions

Most people think of emotions as wide reaching—we have joy and delight and excitement, but in reality, they are all subsets of just seven universal emotions. These emotions are universal because we can identify them in all cultures around the world—even people born blind who have never actually seen a human face before still exhibit these emotions accurately and with the right facial expressions, leading to the belief that these emotions are innate rather than created through learning.

The seven emotions that are deemed universal in humans include:

- **Happiness:** This is the rewarding emotion that you feel when you do something good or right. It is meant to encourage you to repeat those behaviors in the future.

- **Sadness:** Sadness occurs when you do something wrong. It is the emotion that comes along with intense suffering, in which something was lost. It is meant to reinforce that a behavior should not be repeated.

- **Anger:** Anger is necessary to protect yourself—it is there so that you will be able to prevent yourself from any problems with violence. When you are threatened, you will get angry so that you can protect yourself.

- **Fear:** Fear is meant to influence you to run away from a situation to protect yourself. It is the precursor to anger and directly related to the fight or flight response in people. Fear is considered flight, while anger is considered the fight response.

- **Disgust:** Disgust is meant to keep you from consuming something that is toxic or unhealthy for you. When you feel disgusted, your body feels like it is repulsed by something—it wants to get away. This is meant to prevent you from eating, for example, rotten meat.

- **Surprise:** This is meant to redirect your attention and make you focus. When you feel surprised, you stop and look at what is happening around you and identify whatever it was that was not quite right and caught you by surprise.

- **Contempt:** Contempt is sort of like anger meets disgust—it is meant to be an emotion that makes you want nothing to do with someone. Effectively, it makes you look down on someone, unwilling to spend time with that individual any longer.

Defining empathy

With emotions out of the way, let's take a look at empathy. This is one of the defining features of the empath—they are highly empathetic, but what does that mean? Empathy is commonly accepted as the ability of someone to sense the emotions of someone else, as well as being able to understand, to some degree, what the other person is most likely feeling or thinking. It can be physical or emotional. It can involve understanding the position that someone else is in, or it can involve being able to feel their emotions yourself. There are all sorts of ways in which empathy plays out, and they all vary greatly from each other.

Empathy is incredibly important—it teaches us how to cooperate with each other. It helps us to create friendships or to make decisions that are moral and fair. It helps us help other people who are in need, and we can start to see signs of empathy in even young children and infants. It is there for a very good reason. In particular, it is believed that empathy may have evolved for a very specific reason—in particular, it is there to help to facilitate communication between people. It behaves as a sort of social signal to other people—you can communicate nonverbally when everyone is on the same page.

Think about it—if you are out walking and you see someone threatening behind a tree, but your friends in the group that are just a bit behind you cannot see them, what is the appropriate thing to do? You will probably freeze up at the sight of someone else as your body processes what to do next—and your friends that are behind you, being empathetic, can pick up on the fact that you are afraid, and it puts them on high alert. Now, they are aware that there is a problem instead of walking in blindly to a situation that could be potentially dangerous.

Humans are a social species, and because of that, we need to consider that nonverbal communication is highly important. This is why we have so many physical cues in general—human body language is highly complex. We are able to communicate nonverbally in all sorts of manners, and empathy tends to help with that. It also aids in bonding as well as cooperative behavior so that, as social animals, we are able to communicate even if we cannot use words.

The types of empathy

Empathy comes in all sorts of forms as well, but it is typically broken down into just three different types:

- **Cognitive empathy:** This is being able to know how someone else is feeling and what they may be thinking about at that moment. It is often also referred to as perspective taking. It is thinking and understanding what is going on. Think of this as if you stopped to negotiate something for work. If you notice that the other person's body language is closed off, you will get that sense that they are not feeling very open through cognitive empathy. You will think, "Wow! That person is not very open at all. What can I do to fix this problem?"

- **Emotional empathy:** This form of empathy is a bit different—it concerns itself with the feelings and sensations of someone else. This is where those mirror neurons come into play. When you look at someone else, you will then physically feel the other person's emotions as your own. Your own mirror neurons activate, and you suddenly feel those same feelings.

- **Compassionate empathy:** Finally, we take a look at compassionate empathy. This is the idea that you are able to feel the emotions that someone else is feeling while still being able to cognitively understand what they are thinking as well. It takes both the cognitive and compassionate sides and puts them together to create action.

Rationality Vs. Emotionality

You have all sorts of emotions for varying reasons. However, one thing is certain—your thoughts influence your emotions, and your emotions influence your behaviors. When you consider this endless cycle of thoughts, emotions, and behaviors, you realize that you have a method of controlling them built into this cycle. With thoughts, you can tame your emotions.

We typically can behave either rationally or emotionally at any point in time. Typically, you cannot rationally behave emotionally—they are like two ends of a spectrum. However, you can learn to recognize both the importance of logic and rationality while still being an emotional person. It is well within your power to be able to feel those emotions and let them act as informants about your current situation. Your body feels those emotions for a reason, after all, and if you can identify why you feel those ways, you can use those interpretations to respond logically and responsibly. You could, for example, tell yourself that you are feeling scared because you realize that you are walking in an area in which you got into a car accident a year prior. When you identify the reason for those emotions, the emotions lose power to the rationality.

This is where stoicism and empathy will come into play together—you can use them at the same time, allowing for your empathy to let those emotions play their roles while still making sure that you are able to rationalize what is happening at the same time. You can think about the emotions. You can identify why you have those emotions. When you do that, you realize that you have more skills and capabilities than you ever realized. You can defeat that need to behave emotionally. You can remove the need for you to feel like you are a slave to your passions, something that we will be discussing very deeply later in this book as we tackle stoicism.

Introducing the Empath

Elysia is a 20-years-old college student studying social work. She is highly empathetic—she has not once seen a movie where someone died without tearing up or sometimes even crying. She feels sad when her friends around her are sad, and she also picks up on tension as soon as she walks through the door. Of course, that worked both ways—sometimes, she would be surrounded by positive, happy people and couldn't feel better. She loved it when she was able to enjoy other people around her or when the energy in a room was just right. Elysia never figured out quite how to explain the way that she felt... Until the day that she stumbled upon the word *empath* online.

Highly sensitive. Attuned to the emotions of others. Struggles with personal boundaries. The more that she read the traits of the empath, the more it made sense—she was also a highly sensitive empath.

Elysia struggled with her boundaries. She would often let people walk all over her because she would rather sacrifice herself than make someone else unhappy. She regularly allowed other people to rule over her. She allowed all sorts of transgressions to slide because she feared rocking the boat too much or making other people miserable. As an empath, she had some serious work to do if she wanted to be able to get through life without letting every negative emotion, she passed wash over her.

Empaths are often defined as too sensitive or emotional. They are typically identified by being told that they need to calm down or stop reacting so much. However, that is not entirely fair to accuse them of. Empaths themselves are people who are highly sensitive—in particular, they are highly sensitive to the emotions and potentially even the thoughts of those around them. They are usually able to pick up on signs that most people do not realize, and because they are able to do so, they also unintentionally tend to make themselves suffer as well. They often take on the emotions of the people around them as well, which is where that reputation comes in. When a highly sensitive person is in a room full of bad energy or vibes, they usually feel miserable. They feel stressed out or annoyed with the interactions that they are getting, and because of that, they start to struggle with their emotions. For the empath, it is difficult to define where their emotions begin and where they end. However, it is highly possible to understand those differences over time. It is quite simple to be able to define where those feelings start and end if you learn how to do so, and that is a critical skill for all empaths to know.

Introducing Stoicism

John is a quiet 27-years old man. He tries to remind himself that keeping himself rooted firmly in the realm of logic is the best way to control himself. We are, after all, cognitively rational creatures. We are designed to have this ability—but we have to make sure that we make it a point to tap into it, after all. He spends his time working diligently without complaint. Even when he is asked to stay late, he is willing to put in that effort. Even when he doesn't want to, he is happy to do so because he knows that it is for the best.

Most of John's friends would describe him as cold or unfeeling, but that could not be further from the truth—he is quite emotional, but he makes sure that is mind is in control at all times. He understands that we have emotions and that they have a purpose, but more than anything else, he also recognizes that he is able to influence and control those emotions so that he is able to control himself as well.

As a Stoic, he was content, knowing that he would be able to control himself. He did know that emotions mattered to him, but usually, he wanted to focus on thinking rationally. After all, we have those passions, and they usually get us into trouble.

Stoicism, and the followers, known as Stoics, are highly rational individuals. They focus on the idea that logic matters more than everything else. Derived from the Greek philosopher, Zeno of Citium, Stoicism focuses on the nature of the soul, learning about the nature of the mind and referring to it as having an internal heat or fire, known as the pneuma, or the soul. The pneuma was identified as being various actions that were performed by the individuals; it was the world-soul; it worked to motivate and drive us.

Stoics, then, attempted to control that pneuma to achieve Eudaimonia—utter happiness or blessedness. Eudaimonia is believed to be achieved through controlling and accepting the moment. This means that, for the Stoic, being able to control oneself is the utmost pleasure. It is to recognize the virtue within humans—the good deeds that we do. It rejects the idea that you must have external material belongings to be happy.

To the Stoics, they recognize the world as being an amalgamation of logic, physics, and naturalistic ethics, focusing on human knowledge and what we have control over. It focuses on developing the self through being able to teach and fortify oneself against those destructive emotions that will otherwise cause problems, and through this path, it is possible to overcome everything.

Who Is the Stoic Empath?

When you look at the two, it is easy to see why so many people may believe in that false dichotomy—you see that the empaths are highly emotional, but at the same time, the Stoics are highly focused on controlling those negative emotions. Where, then, is the line drawn, you may ask?

Notice how the Stoics control their emotions and reactions while the empath feels them deeply. There is nothing about the two that are inherently delegitimizing of the other. It is entirely possible to follow the Stoic way of life while still being an empath, and doing so is actually a great way to achieve power. In fact, Stoicism actually promotes the use of empathy and being empathetic toward other people. It is highly important to the Stoics that people should pay close attention to others, listening to them, and acknowledging that what they say is valid.

Marcus Aurelius, one of the most famous Stoics, wrote that we must be able to pay close attention to what other people are saying, making sure that we are able to, as he put it, "enter[ing], so far as possible, into the mind of the speaker," in his famous *Meditations,* Book 6, line 53. Is that not highly indicative of empathy right there? That is effectively the definition of cognitive empathy, and here is Marcus Aurelius, encouraging it.

It is emphasized even more later as well in his *Meditations*—he also discusses, in book 7, line 4, that "In conversation, one should attend closely to what is being said, and with regard to every impulse attend to what arises from it; in the latter case, to see from the first what end it has in view, and in the former, to keep a careful watch on what people mean to say." He is effectively encouraging the followers of Stoicism to not only pay attention to the words that are being said but also paying close attention to the way that it is said. It advocates for paying attention to the impulse—the emotions—behind the actions and the words. He is pushing the point that we should all be looking at each other empathetically, even in stoicism, for when we can identify the way that other people are feeling, we can then begin to see the truth of what was meant to be said. We are able to understand deeper, to be able to comprehend the truest intentions of the words being said.

The Stoic empath, then, is someone who does this—it is someone who is following the truths of Stoicism, following those principles and making sure to live the life working toward virtue, while still recognizing that emotions are important. They can see exactly what value comes from emotions and being able to use them, and they tend to encourage the usage of those emotions so that they can get the most out of the situation.

Chapter 2: Understanding the Empath

Empathy is to make ourselves vulnerable and open—it is to welcome in the emotions of others, no matter what they are. Sometimes, this can be highly inconvenient; when it happens, you can unintentionally find yourself in a bad spot in which you are stuck with someone else's bad emotions, and that can be difficult to deal with. Empathy, however, is also highly powerful. It is healing. It helps us to reach out to others, to connect, and to be able to really understand the situations of others, to develop that compassion and desire to help. Some of the most kindhearted people in the world are empaths, highly driven by their desire to help other people because they can feel those emotions emanating off of people, and it hurts. They see someone who is hungry on the side of the road with a sign, and they want to cry. They want to be able to relate better. They want to connect, even when it feels like it is too much. However, the empaths sometimes get burnt out after a while; after enough time, they start to feel like they are too emotional, or they cannot cope with the negative or foreign emotions that they are filled with.

As we read through this chapter, we are going to be taking a look at some of the most common traits of the empath to get a better understanding of who they are, what they do, and how they behave. If you can understand this as an empath, you can start to see some of the traits that you may never have even realized that you possess. These traits and emotions are highly influential and can even be overwhelming ad annoying sometimes, but they are important to recognize so that you do understand the ways that you engage with the world around you. The more that you begin to understand how you navigate through the world, the sooner that you can start to fix the actions that are not beneficial to you—and stoicism later can actually help you greatly with doing so.

Now, let's take a look at nine of the most major traits of empaths in general. Keep in mind that these are generalizations of the empath specifically—they are not specific to empathy itself, but rather to the highly sensitive empath.

Empaths Absorb Emotions

Empaths, by definition, are highly empathetic to *something*. Most of them are particularly in tune with the emotions of other people—they find themselves driven specifically by the feelings that other people have at any point in time and take on the emotions of others. This is believed to be caused by overactive mirror neurons—the neurons that are responsible for the empathizing in people who are not highly empathetic.

Imagine this for a moment—if you walk into a room, does your mood suddenly shift? Do you often find yourself furious when someone else is, or deeply moved when you hear someone else struggling and crying? If you find that your mood usually reflects people around you, there is a good chance that you are empathic, and that can bring with it its own handful of struggles if you are not careful. You will need to make sure that, when you do interact with people, you pay special attention to the emotions of other people, and you must always make sure that you ask yourself if you are feeling the emotions of someone else or if you are feeling your own.

Think of emotions, for empaths, as highly contagious—the emotional contagion highly impacts them and renders them entirely caught up in what they are doing. They get stuck with the emotions of the people around them, and they cannot do anything about it. However, they can learn to differentiate themselves from those emotions so that they can do better.

Empaths Struggle in Public

Because empaths tend to absorb the emotions of other people, they typically struggle greatly when it comes to getting out in public. The public can be highly overwhelming for them, and they can feel like they are stuck. They can feel overwhelmed by the constant inundation of emotions from strangers walking by. Because they are highly empathetic to people, they pick up those feelings as they go by.

When this happens, they can feel like they are getting emotional whiplash; it is possible that the emotions are constantly swirling around, draining the empath until they can no longer tolerate being out in those crowds, and they need to retreat. This typically garners empaths with the designation of introverted—people who find that being around other people is highly draining.

Think of it like going into public is like running a marathon. You must constantly be fending off all of those negative feelings as you go through your day, and that can be entirely overwhelming. It can be difficult at times to even tell if the mood that you are feeling is your own or someone else's, and because of that, it can be tough to figure out how to react and how to treat those around you. You may end up with a reputation of being too reactive or too unstable when, in reality, you were just responding to the world around you.

Empaths Feel the Energy in the Room

If you are not an empath, you may not quite understand this one, but any empath will know immediately what is meant by this. When you walk into a room as an empath, you will feel the energy in the room immediately. You cannot help it—all around you; you feel the constant energy from people. You do not need to talk to anyone to tell the mood when you first enter the room in the first place. When you enter, you simply begin to pick up on the cues enough to understand what you will need to know if you want to mesh with the group.

The empaths will almost always read the mood of a room just right. They pick it up on their own, subconsciously picking up all of the body language in the room and taking it on as their own. As their mirror neurons activate when they enter the room, they pick up on tensions if they are high. They can see when people are having a good time or struggling to have a difficult conversation, even if there is nothing readily apparent externally that will betray what is being discussed.

Empaths Understand the Perspectives of Others

Because of the skills that empaths have when it comes to reading the feelings of others, they are also able to pick up on perspectives readily and easily. This is a great benefit, but also a major struggle at the same time. As an empath, you will be able to tell why people are doing what they are doing. You never judge people for their actions—rather, you take time to understand the background information as well.

Think of a situation in which you may have seen someone do something that was, objectively speaking, wrong. Maybe they stole a loaf of bread or a gallon of milk from the grocery store, but they were caught as they tried to leave. When you hear the man sobbing about how hungry his toddler is, you can't help but feel bad for him. Did he do a bad thing? Absolutely—stealing is, objectively speaking, and legally speaking, verboten. You know that it is not allowed, but still, you do not feel like the person is a bad one. You know that his heart was in the right place—he wasn't out there stealing lobster and cigarettes or alcohol—he was stealing basic supplies for his young, hungry child ad you could not find any real way to fault him for that, even though you knew it was wrong.

Taking the perspective of other people can be a great asset, but it can also come back to cause problems if you are not careful.

Empaths Attract People in Need of Help

More often than not, empaths have a way of attracting people who are in need of help. They are simply approachable, and while they may not like to admit it or to deal with it in the moment, they are usually happy to help—helping is in their nature, and they struggle to turn away someone in need of assistance for any reason.

Whether for advice that is needed, such as about a difficult topic or something about how to react to someone else, or even just needing directions, something about empaths is warm and inviting to those needing something. Empaths, despite typically being quite reserved, find themselves constantly approached for all sorts of reasons, to the point where they assume that it is normal to be approached—until their friends mention that it is strange how often they are approached on the regular.

Empaths are also typically highly supportive of people, and that can attract even more people to them. They are usually willing and ready to listen, even if it is something difficult for them to deal with. Of course, that usually then leads to drained energy reserves and feeling burnt out at the end of the day as well. However, the empath will do it anyway to help those in need.

Empaths Struggle With Difficult News

When empaths are exposed to difficult news, they tend to struggle. They may see that someone was in a horrible accident and start to cry for them—even though they have no true idea who the individual was. They may never have even heard of that individual, but they still struggled to cope with the news. For empaths, hearing about people suffering, no matter what happened to lead up to it, is too much.

Empaths may get upset at hearing about violence, and when it comes to hearing bad news from one of their friends and family members, they struggle to cope with it. They find that it is just too much to bear, and it can be incredibly draining for them. Oftentimes, the negative news can cause them to feel strong emotions even when really, there is no direct impact on them. This sensitivity has its pace, but it can also be difficult to deal with. Any sort of tragedy is painful, real, or fictional. Any sort of television shows, even where it is clearly fiction, is enough to bring on the waterworks. It can be difficult to watch sometimes, and empaths sometimes even go out of their ways to avoid the content if they can when they find it to be too emotionally triggering. They would rather simply remain out of the loop than continue to suffer with it.

Empaths Love Pets and Babies

While empaths typically struggle with adults and the emotions that they bring, they typically find solace in the company of both babies and pets. There is just something about the pure, unbridled joy of both pets and babies that can be quite recharging and even relaxing and bring them the peace that they may need after a long, hard day of dealing with the emotions of other people.

Empaths Struggle With Emotional Contagion

For empaths, emotional contagion is very real. You can see this oftentimes in even babies—it has been found that if one newborn in a hospital ward starts to cry, the whole ward may start to cry in return. One person talking about their anxiety can also start everyone else to feel anxiety as well. However, for the empaths, it is worse—it is more intense and difficult to cope with. They struggle to deal with the negativity that they sometimes get from other people. They know that it is not good for them, but they often struggle to really identify in the moment whether the emotions belong to them or to someone else.

The emotions that the empath feels are real, even if they are not theirs in origin. They still feel the same strong emotions going through them. They still have the same physical reaction that other people have, but they simply did not share the same cause. However, that does not mean that you can just tell an empath to get over it and move on, or to stop overreacting. Rather, you have to support them and make sure that they understand that it is valid to feel such strong emotions no matter what.

Empaths Struggle in Relationships

Another common trait of the empath is struggling in relationships. For empaths, they find that it is difficult to keep themselves separate from their partners—they struggle to maintain those fine boundaries between themselves and other people. As those boundaries blur, it gets harder to make sure that you are maintaining your own privacy or your own personality. For many empaths, it can be easy to get caught up in the idea that you have to take on the same likes, opinions, and general thoughts as the other people. This is exacerbated by the fact that you may spend longer periods of time with your partner, especially if you live together. It is natural for you, as an empath, to start to get caught up in their emotions and thoughts without thinking about it. However, it is highly important that you are able to make sure that you keep your own autonomy. Boundaries have to be maintained, and when they start to fall, there are very real problems.

Empaths Are Easy Targets for Abuse

Because of the fact that empaths are so emotionally available for everyone around them and they naturally try to see the best in everyone, trying to take on the perspectives of other people rather than taking a look at a situation based on black and white views of a situation, they are very easy to take advantage of. People who are highly empathetic usually try to listen to all of the potential excuses that are supposed to be there to justify the abuse that they are experiencing. They may tell themselves that it is not the fault of the abuser that they are repeating behaviors that they learned growing up, or they may tell themselves that really, the abuse was their fault, not the fault of the abuser. They are so empathetic and so desperate to see the good in other people that they tend to forget that ultimately, they are not responsible for everyone around them. There are no rules that say that they must be responsible for every little thing that happens to them—in fact, it is the opposite. They must learn to recognize that they are at risk of becoming codependent if they are not careful.

Empaths Need Time Alone

Finally, a very common trait of an empath is the need for alone time—they need to spend time away from other people so that they can relax and recharge. The alone time is crucial, and they may even say that they need to be left alone from their partners as well, sometimes. This is not because they dislike the people around them—they just need a respite from feeling everyone else's feelings as well. It can be highly overwhelming to constantly feel what everyone else is feeling around them. If you are an empath, make sure that you get that time for yourself. If you know an empath, always respect when they ask for that privacy.

Chapter 3: Pros and Cons of the Empath's Power

Now, it may seem like being an empath is more of a problem than a blessing, and in many ways, it can be. However, the empathic abilities of someone else are not a curse—they are a blessing, and they need to be treated in that manner. It may take you some time to get to know those feelings and abilities for what they really are, but if you can get used to the way that you think or adjust yourself to the interactions that you have with other people, you will find that being empathetic can actually be both one of your greatest assets and worst weaknesses that you have.

It is very important for you to understand what it means to be and live as an empath. It is hard to identify the empath sometimes, but when they are identified, usually, you can figure out that they actually have some pretty wonderful abilities that they may not usually advertise or broadcast widely. Yes, being empathic can have some cons—but so can anything else. It is normal for something to have pros and cons, and it is next to impossible to ever have something that is completely free of any negative aspects. We are not perfect beings—we all have our pros and cons. We all have our strengths and weaknesses, but it is when you learn to identify them and use them that you will be able to really begin to understand yourself.

Pros to Being an Empath

Being an empath is not all bad—not by a long shot. There are many different skills and traits related to being an empath that can actually be quite beneficial if you can learn to harness them. Your abilities are a gift, and these are the ways that you can count on your powers to benefit you at some point in your life.

You are strongly in tune with the emotions of others

When you are able to pay attention to how other people feel, and you are able to pick up on those emotions without having to try, you can take advantage of that fact. There are many different situations in which you will be able to make use of reading the emotions of other people—it is highly beneficial if, for example, you have to work with people. Imagine that you are a salesperson for a moment. If you can read other people with ease, you can start to make use of that. You can change your own behaviors to try to influence other people.

We are naturally social beings, after all, and we tend to interact closely with each other.

If you notice that someone is nervous about closing the deal, for example, you can be more reassuring, offering all of the necessary evidence to show them that they do not have to worry so much. If the other person is too closed off to get very far in negotiations, you can work to open them up to make sure that they actually want to be willing to close the deal. You will be able to make use of your skills to help other people in these ways.

Alternatively, you will also be able to pick up on dangerous situations. If the feelings that you pick up on are bad enough, you can usually figure out why and you will then be able to react accordingly. If someone is giving you bad vibes, there is probably a reason for it. Trust your gut, empath—it is almost always right.

You love and feel compassion deeper than the average person

Your emotions are also quite magnified when you are empathic. This is not because of anything that you do—rather, you simply tend to love and feel compassion more than other people. This is something that is difficult for empaths to deal with, but it should be accepted as genuine. In fact, the amount of love and compassion that you feel can even be almost overwhelming sometimes.

As an empath, the feelings that you have are intense, and they will be further magnified when you catch onto the feelings of your partner as well. It can be difficult for the empath to navigate relationships with others just due to the sheer extreme level of interaction that you have in relationships and just how overwhelming they can become, but when you are able to embrace and harness that propensity for love and compassion, you can get far in life.

That compassion can also be channeled toward work as well—many empaths naturally find themselves wanting to find a job in which they are able to help other people as much as possible. They are driven to become the teachers for tomorrow's generation. They want to become social workers to help other people escape abusive situations or break free from poverty's grasp. They want to make sure that they are able to do the most good in the world as possible—even if that comes with the territory of being surrounded by people that are too difficult to be around, or being around hard emotions to handle.

You are a fantastic judge of character

When you first meet someone or even get into a situation that stirs strong emotions in you, you learn pretty quickly to trust those gut reactions. You are fantastic at judging the character of people just because of the fact that you are so in tune with everyone around you. You may catch onto things that you cannot understand why you know them. You may realize that you are asking questions that are related to a specific trauma. You may ask them if they are struggling with something that is entirely related to what you are talking about—because you have a hunch, and you have to find out if you are right.

Likewise, you are likely to find that your strong negative impulses or assumptions are right as well. If you feel that someone is going to be a bad idea to hang around, you should probably trust that gut instinct—it is there for a reason, and it is not going to steer you wrong. Empaths can sense the intentions of other people; they can tell when someone is approaching them with the intention to harm them or to be kind. This sort of internal radar can be incredibly useful for you when you are out and about. The intuition that you have is incredible and one of the greatest tools that you can have.

You can identify liars

You will be able to tell when someone is lying. It can be kind of hard to explain, but you may get a feeling in your gut that the other person is lying, whether they have indicated that they are lying or not. This is quite powerful—if you need to talk to people and get honesty for work, this is a great way to do so. If you want to make sure that you are not being lied to, you will be able to do that.

Of course, this has other implications as well—if you can tell when someone is lying to you, you are going to be able to protect yourself. If you can tell that someone else is trying to manipulate you, you can break free from that—you can tell yourself that you will not be tolerating that kind of behavior and refuse to engage with it. You will be able to follow that intuition, and if you do not, you will probably learn pretty quickly that you should have listened to it the first time.

Cons to Being an Empath

Of course, there are also all sorts of cons to being highly empathic as well, but those can be worked through with time. Make sure that you are acutely aware of the cons that you are likely to face—when you know what your weaknesses are, you will be able to guard against them and prevent these cons from actually controlling you. When you learn to protect yourself, these cons will not be nearly as bad as they would be if you left them entirely unguarded—learn to recognize the warning signs and respect them for what they are so that you can protect yourself, no matter what happens.

You feel the emotions of other people

Any empath would readily admit that the ability to feel the emotions of other people is both a blessing and a curse. It is great when you are able to use it, but sometimes, you can become overwhelmed. When you are constantly being impacted by the emotions of other people, you can find that it is difficult to concentrate. It can be draining, and even dangerous sometimes if you are constantly struggling with emotions.

You can even start to pick up strongly negative emotions as well—and those can leave you reeling and really struggling to interact well with people around you. If you are particularly sensitive, you may find that you are caught up in the anxiety or depression of other people, suffering from pain that is not yours, nor does it originate from you. Yes, you can use that information that you have to try to help yourself, but at the end of the day, you must remember that you have to protect yourself and your emotions. You need to be able to keep in mind that if your emotions are running high, you need to stop yourself and ask if they are yours or someone else's.

You are more likely to be overwhelmed

When you are highly sensitive, you are much more likely to get overwhelmed. This makes sense—you cannot push back at those negative emotions to protect yourself. They simply fester and eat at you until they are too much for you to bear. When you have no real way to stop those emotions, you find that you have to take other approaches instead, and that can be difficult sometimes when you are entirely unsure of how to change up your reactions.

Beyond just emotions, you are also likely to be highly susceptible to being overwhelmed by all sorts of other aspects of life as well. It could be that touch sets you off, or you could struggle with louder noises. Highly sensitive people can be sensitive to more than just emotions—senses can be overwhelming as well, and that sensitivity can make it so that you cannot properly cope with the struggles that you have at any point in time. It is also possible that your sensitivity can actually make you more susceptible to panic attacks and higher levels of anxiety as well, especially in situations in which you are struggling greatly with dealing with the emotions of other people.

You have mood swings

When you are empathic, you are likely to find that your emotions swing from end to end on the spectrum—you cannot help it; it happens on its own, and it can be incredibly detrimental to you and those around you. When you struggle to control your own mood because you are constantly reflecting the moods of other people, you can really struggle with yourself. You will be stuck, feeling entire as if you are a slave to those intense emotions if you are not careful. Your emotions will become your worst enemy as an empath if you cannot learn to manage them, and that is one of the hardest things for you to do.

Even worse, you will probably struggle to know which emotions are yours and which are those of other people. This means that, if you are inexperienced, you will probably find yourself wondering if you actually feel the way that you are feeling or if you are reflecting the feelings of other people—and it will oftentimes be kind of hard to tell the difference. However, you can learn to do exactly that if you work hard to protect yourself.

You may be more susceptible to using drugs or alcohol

Being empathic is draining for the best of us. It is utterly destructive for those who do not know what they are doing or for those who are unsure of how to approach the problem in the first place. All too often, people who are desperate for a respite from the constant inundation of emotion may find themselves instead shifting to drinking or using drugs in an attempt to escape the pain that comes along with the empathic nature of your mind.

Of course, unhealthy coping mechanisms are not going to help you at all—they are actually only going to make things worse. You need to make sure that you are able to make use of the right, healthier coping mechanisms that will help to take that edge off without having to resort to alcohol or drugs. You can learn to do it, and we will be going over some of these methods in the next chapter that you can use to protect yourself.

You are physically exhausted

As much as you are emotionally exhausted by your empathic abilities, you may be surprised to realize that you become physically drained as well—you may find that the emotions that you feel get so strong and overwhelming sometimes that you cannot help but feel that you are physically exhausted as well. This often happens in particular after becoming unable to cope with the sheer level of stimulation emotionally that you have received. The overstimulation drives you insane and makes it impossible for you to cope further. When this happens, you will need to find some other way for you to cope.

You may also have physical symptoms related to your physical exhaustion as well. Commonly, empaths will struggle with migraines or headaches, and may even suffer from their ears ringing as well. It is a sign that you have taken on too much and that you will need to recharge.

You are a common target for abuse

All sorts of people want to take advantage of you when you are highly empathic. This is because they can sense that you are the kind of person to whom they can give the benefit of the doubt, and therefore, it will be very easy to walk all over. When it comes right down to it, your empathic tendencies to be kind to everyone and to give everyone that you meet the benefit of the doubt can be quite harmful to you and works to essentially enable your abusers or those that are trying to manipulate you. You must learn to recognize that, even if you would never use someone else, other people are willing to be opportunistic and take any chance that they can get to take control of someone else for their own benefit.

Chapter 4: Protecting the Empathic Self

If you are an empath, you know the pain of being in a room that is just a bit too busy for you. You know the feeling of doubt, of your gut gnawing at itself because of what you are able to sense around you. You will be able to feel these intense feelings within you, stressing you out and putting you on edge. However, you do not have to feel these ways. You can learn to protect yourself so that you can avoid that constant discomfort.

Keep in mind that there is no such thing as a cure for the empath, nor is there any way for you to simply never be inconvenienced by the problem that you are having with absorbing the energy of others. However, recognize that you must make sure that you are able to protect yourself to lessen some of that drain. If you can lessen the drain, you can start to protect yourself from becoming overstimulated so that you can leave and find somewhere that you can recharge when the time is there.

As you read through these activities and methods that you can use to protect yourself from being completely overwhelmed by the energies around you, keep in mind that you will need to work well with yourself to protect yourself from suffering. Keep in mind that it will be a trial and error period while you figure out what works and what you prefer not to do. You need to figure out what will be the most beneficial to you and you alone and make sure that you always respect that need to escape when you need it. These methods will help to protect you, but you will still be susceptible to being drained.

Shielding Visualization

Shielding is a very popular method that empaths use to help them fortify themselves against the feelings of others that threaten to overwhelm them. When you are able to use shielding, you can effectively block out the toxic energy so that you are able to focus only on the positivity instead, protecting yourself and keeping up the energy that you want to absorb while rejecting the toxic stuff that is going to drain you faster than anything else.

This is a method that can be used anywhere, and you should do so any time that you feel like you need it. If you feel like you are in a bad spot suddenly, if you start to pick up on those bad vibes, it is time to summon that shield to protect yourself, and you can do this incredibly simple. All you have to do is become aware of the negative situation, trust yourself, and begin to visualize.

Take a few deep breaths, in and out, breathing slowly as you do. After a few deep breaths, imagine that there is a shield beginning to form around you. It could create a barrier in a great, big bubble around you, or it could be against your skin, protecting your body from the negative energy surrounding you. The shield should be protective and comforting. Visualize it to be beautiful and warm, and then imagine that it extends out just past you, at least a few inches away. As you do this, visualize the negative energy bouncing right off of it and away into the universe. As you do this, you will be able to keep yourself centered. You will remind yourself that you are not feeling any negative emotions at that moment, and you will be able to reject them as not being yours. Likewise, you will be able to feel centered and energized as you do this. It will keep you safe and comfortable, even if you are somewhere that you would otherwise be stressed out by.

Expressing Your Needs

In relationships, it is very easy to get completely overwhelmed. It is difficult to put yourself first when you are an empath, and because of that, you may really struggle to help yourself figure out how to express what you want or what you need. You might struggle to assert those needs, even if you know that there will be no resistance over them if you were to mention them. You must make sure that you learn how you can express them with your partner so that you will be able to protect and care for yourself.

Keep in mind that, in a healthy relationship, your partner *wants* to know what it will take to keep you comfortable. Your partner *wants* you to be taken care of. Your partner does not want you to suffer. Because of this, you need to learn to find your voice. You need to learn to tell your partner what you need so that you do not suffer.

Start this by asking yourself what you need. What is it that you have been afraid to ask for? Do you need more time by yourself, or spent together? Do you need to find ways to engage with each other more? Be honest with each other and express those needs without any judgment. Let your partner know exactly how you feel. It will be harder at first, but over time, you can master this art and make sure that you are giving yourself and your partner the respect and relationship that you both deserve.

Setting Boundaries

Whether at home or at work, boundaries and empaths rarely mesh well, especially if the empath is not fully comfortable in his or her powers at that point in time. However, boundaries are essential. Like shielding, you can create a sort of barrier through which you block out the stress and protect your energy level. A common method to do this is to make use of a few small trinkets or items that have a deep meaning to you and then place them along the perimeter of the space that you are in.

For example, imagine that you are at work and your office tends to stress you out. Instead of giving into that stress, you decide that you are going to focus on blocking the stress out. You take a picture of your partner, or of your children, if applicable, and you place them on the edge of your desk. You can put objects that have a deep meaning as well—you could have, for example, a small stone that you keep on your desk or a religious object for the religion that you practice and place them at the edge of your desk. Plants are another common one that is used for the empath, creating a protective boundary that they can rely on to help them.

This effectively helps them to mute out any of the stress that is surrounding them. They are able to create an area in which they are willing to be entirely at ease at work or at home.

Preventing Overload

You must also be well aware of how you can prevent yourself from suffering from empathy overload. Empathy overload is that state at which you can no longer fight against the negativity that you are feeling—it is so overwhelming that it takes over, and you need to find some way to protect yourself.

However, if you can prevent yourself from getting to that overloaded state, you can prevent the meltdown that will otherwise come. If you are aware of the fact that you are absorbing stress, you can stop yourself from being able to release the negative energy. Some people will make use of essential oils, and others will make it a point to meditate or breathe deeply, imagining that as they breathe out, they are releasing their stressors and protecting themselves. No matter how you choose to do it, you are usually able to start feeling better quickly.

Make sure that in preventing overload, you need to balance the time that you spend with other people versus spending time with those around you. You want to make sure that the time that you spend with other people is highly effective, and this means that you need to also give yourself that recharge time on the regular. The only person that is going to protect you from burnout is yourself. This means that you must be mindful of your schedule and do not be afraid to reschedule if you have to.

Further, make sure that you make it a point to set clear boundaries with people that you know are toxic. You are allowed to say no to people, and even better, you owe nobody an explanation for why you are saying no in the first place. You do not have to justify why you will say no. Also, you must make sure that when you are trying to protect yourself from those meltdowns, you shield yourself effectively. Practice self-care and make sure that you are kind to yourself. Remind yourself that sometimes, the best that you can do is good enough, even if you did not get what you were trying to do done.

The Empathic Protector Meditation

When you need some extra guidance or another shield, a common meditation is to call upon a protector for yourself. Imagine this as being akin to your spirit animal or spiritual guide—it should be something that speaks to you spiritually, that makes you feel at ease. Some people like to use wolves or tigers. Others prefer smaller animals. Whatever it is, it should be something that can protect you and that you can envision fighting off the pain or negativity that is filling your heart. If you find that you are being overwhelmed rapidly with negativity before you are able to keep it out or protect yourself, try to make use of this meditation.

First, you must figure out what it is that you want to visualize. What kind of animal speaks to your heart? What do you feel an affinity for? Imagine that anima in the depths of your heart manifested of your very soul. When you are overwhelmed or teetering on the edge of becoming overwhelmed, stop, take a deep breath, and summon the image in your mind's eye.

As you summon that image of the great, big predator that is there to protect you, you can start to imagine it protecting you. Make sure that it carefully and thoroughly guards you; it should walk around you. It should make sure that none of that overwhelmingly negative energy gets through to you. It is patient. It is powerful. And, it can destroy and dissolve that negative energy for you.

Imagine that the protector is shielding you and protecting you. Imagine how it looks, how it looks to you, protecting you, and ensuring that you are not afraid. Imagine how it cares for you and how it looks to you like it can keep you safe. Feel the strength of the creature filling you and keeping you capable of continuing forward. Imagine that you are entirely protected.

This is something that you should be able to use at any moment. Save it for the last resort—whenever you are overwhelmed, or risking that point of being overwhelmed, use it. If you can keep it special and calming for you, you will be able to keep yourself steady no matter what you are facing.

Journal Regularly

As an empath, you probably fill up on negative energy on a regular basis, even if you do everything in your power not to. That energy has to be processed somehow, and a great way to do so is through the use of journaling. When you journal, you can protect yourself from those negative emotions. When you journal, you can release them out and begin to work through the thoughts that are circling around in your mind. You will be channeling the energy in your mind and heart to the paper, and in doing so, you get that power back over the situation.

Take the time every day to do this—spend time at night, preferably just before bed, releasing all of that pent up negativity so that you can be free of it for a restful sleep. When you do this, you are able to start relaxing over time. Being able to release that energy will help with your sleep and your mood, and you will be able to use it on a regular basis.

Avoid Toxic People

This should go without saying, but one of the greatest things that you can do for yourself as an empath is to make sure that you avoid anyone that is toxic. Make sure that, no matter what is happening, you make sure that you are paying close attention to the people around you. Make sure that you are avoiding the people in your life that are going to do nothing but harm you or bring you down. When you notice who the true toxic individuals are, from the narcissists to the abusers or anyone else that just wants to take advantage of you, you need to get away. You need to find ways that you can protect yourself, and for most people, that involves figuring out how to escape them and how you can stay away.

Remember this—no one is entitled to your time. No one is entitled to controlling or using you. No one is worth sacrificing everything for if all they want to do is take advantage of you. Respect yourself. Remember that you are valuable as well, and make sure that you protect yourself and your mind. If you feel like someone else seems dangerous, there is probably a reason for it. Do not let yourself fall for those traps of trying to justify it—negativity and toxicity are negative and toxic for a reason. You wouldn't let a rattlesnake bite you just because it asked nicely, would you? So why let a toxic individual subject you to their negativity and potentially violence without a good reason to do so? Your only duty is to yourself, and you must do what it will take to protect yourself, even if that means cutting people off, regardless of who they are. There is no reason to let yourself be subjected to constant negativity, even if they are family.

Chapter 5: Finding Peace and Happiness as an Empath

The empath is sensitive—that cannot be avoided. However, just because you are sensitive and constantly inundated with a wide range of emotions does not mean that you cannot achieve utter happiness. You can learn to be at peace and happy with yourself—you just have to learn what it is that you need. You can learn to find both peace and happiness as an empath, protecting yourself from everything that you will likely experience if you were to not bother. If you know what you are doing, you can ensure that you are highly insulated against the stress and turmoil that emotional contagion can inflict upon you. You just have to learn to know what you are doing.

Within this chapter, we are going to look at what it is that the empath requires for happiness. These are the points and recommendations to remember if you want to be able to achieve and attain that happiness to ensure that ultimately, at the end of the day, you are able to cope with your larger than life feeling that you may sometimes suffer from. The sooner that you learn to overcome those emotions and protect yourself, the sooner that you can begin working to ensure that your thoughts and feelings are valid and able to protect you. All you need to do is follow these steps to achieve that inner peace.

Spend Time Alone

When you spend time alone as the empathic individual that you are, you are able to remind yourself that ultimately, you can recover. As someone that is highly reactive, you will want to make sure that you have the time where you are able to get away from everyone around you. It lets you stop and think about yourself and your reactions. It is easy to feel so caught up in the world around us that we cannot identify our own feelings. It is imperative that you are able to figure out exactly what you need to be happy so that you can, in fact, achieve it regularly, and oftentimes, that comes with the time alone to reflect quietly.

It is difficult to attain peace so that we can reflect when we are surrounded by other people. It is imperative that you are able to spend that time alone so that you can actually get that inner peace. If you want to be happy overall, you need to have the time to relax alone and recharge. You need to be able to spend that time figuring out what it is that you want. It is not only just that you want that time spent alone so that you can recharge—but you also need to be able to think and act accordingly.

Spend Time in Nature

Likewise, spending time in nature is imperative if you want to be happy as an empath. Most empaths find that nature is highly recharging for them. Nature is healing—we are meant to be outdoors, and in order to be happy, empaths require that connection to it in the first place. Being able to take a break from reality and modernity to be present with the plants and animals around is incredibly soothing, and empaths need it to be happy.

Some empaths cope with their need for nature by making sure that they spend time with their own pets. Some will set up home offices or other spaces with the use of all sorts of plants that can help them to feel that connection. Others will make it a point to garden on a regular basis. Others still may prefer to go hiking regularly, away from life. This is healthy for just about anyone—but the empaths, in particular, tend to benefit the most from such activities. You need that peace and quiet. You need the ability to ensure that you are recharging in nature, where you really belong.

If you play your cards right, you can make sure that you interact accordingly. You can spend your time soaking in the healing effects of nature, and the more that you do so, the happier that you will become. If you want to achieve true peace, you must be willing to accommodate accordingly, and that means that you must be willing to spend that time in private in nature, letting it heal you into the healthiest, happiest version of you that you can be.

Have Meaningful Conversations

To be happy, despite being an introvert, you will find that you need meaningful conversations. While introverts are people who are highly drained by interaction, they still enjoy being able to have deep conversations with others. People love being able to interact, and even the introvert is still a social animal—we need connection with others. We crave it, even when we feel like it may destroy us. Without that connection, it is difficult to be able to properly be happy in life.

Introverts, like anyone else, will get lonely at some point. They need to have that connection with other people if they want to be happy, and you must be able to get that somehow. For many people, that comes from deep, meaningful conversations. There is no reason to waste time with small talk for the empath—and most empaths find it too draining to tolerate in the first place. With that in mind, you can see why it becomes imperative to ensure that you are always taking care to find other people that you can have those deep conversations with. Find people that can relate to you that understand what you mean when you want to talk about what matters. Find people who are interested in those discussions about how you should interact or why you should do things a certain way. Find people who like to find out what is on your mind or who want to philosophize about the world with you. It will help you to maintain that happiness.

Spare Yourself From Negative People

Of course, one of the easiest steps that any empath can take to help themselves to maintain positivity and happiness is to make sure that you avoid the negative people in your life. There is literally no reason to keep them around—people known commonly as energy vampires. They are the people who are simply exhausting to be around. When it comes right down to it, they are going to be one of the biggest barriers to happiness just by virtue of the way that they work—the energy vampires in your life are there just to leave you feeling exhausted. They sense that you want nothing more than to help and heal those around you, and they take advantage of it. They see it as a weakness, as something that is worthy of being taken advantage of, and they will do anything in their power to ensure that they come out ahead. People who want to drain you will do so repeatedly and unabashedly as soon as they realize that they have found that in with you.

The best protection that you can have, then, make sure that you avoid those negative, toxic people. When you find that you are constantly being drained by the same people over and over again, feeling like you cannot continue to cope with the interactions much longer, you may be in the presence of an energy vampire. Do they regularly make you do things that you do not want to? Do they pressure you into certain behaviors, knowing that you will give in because they want you to? These are signs that you are near an energy vampire, someone who you should be avoided as much as possible to protect yourself from that sheer exhaustion and drain. You will be so much happier if you do.

Have Partners Who Are Supportive

You should also make sure that in your relationships, you prioritize one fact above all—supportiveness. You want your partners that you have in life to be supportive of you. They should understand what it is to be in a relationship with you. They need to be able to recognize what matters—that you need to ensure that you are taken care of.

It is difficult to be in a relationship as an empath—when you live with someone else, you will find that the entire time that you are with them, you are going to be exposed to someone else's energy. That means that your mind is constantly on overdrive, processing the feelings of other people, and trying to find a way to cope with them. This is difficult for the best of us—it is hard to be able to really focus on yourself when you are feeling the emotions of everyone else first, and because of that, you need to be able to figure out how to cope accordingly.

This means that if you want to be in a happy relationship, you need to be with someone who understands that you need that time to relax and get away. You need to be able to take time to yourself without offending your partner. You need to find someone else who can recognize that your boundaries, physical and personal, will be different from someone who is not highly sensitive.

Practice Mindfulness

When it comes to ensuring that your time and space are recognized and respected, you need to be able to practice mindfulness. Mindfulness should start first thing in the morning and continue around the clock. Everything that you do should be done in the name of mindfulness. Mindfully begin your day. Mindfully go about your day. Mindfully calm yourself down at the end of the day before you go to bed.

Mindfulness is the key to empath happiness—when you are mindful, you can start to better identify when the emotions that you are feeling are your own or when they are those of the other people that you are surrounded by. This means that if you want to be happy and able to succeed in your life, you must be able to see the ways that you interact with other people. You must be able to see when being around people starts to change the emotions that you are feeling as well.

With mindfulness, you can begin to understand the difference between where you end and where everyone else begins—this is imperative if you want to be able to control yourself and that happiness of yours as well. It is not always easy, but an investment in learning to be mindful will go a long way in attaining that long-term happiness for yourself if you know what you are doing.

Acceptance

Acceptance is highly important as an empath. It can be difficult to put up with the emotions running high. It can be tempting to attempt to fight off those emotions somehow or to try to avoid the problem altogether in other ways.

However, if you play your cards right, you can learn to *accept*. This does not mean that you have to simply roll over and take anything that comes your way—rather, you will be learning to make the changes that you can when you can, while still accepting that sometimes, it is what it is and you will have to find a way to cope with that.

Acceptance matters greatly—you need to accept that your feelings will sometimes be running a bit haywire. You need to accept that sometimes, your way of interacting with others is not the preferred method for you. You need to accept that sometimes, your emotions *will* get the best of you, but you still need to find a way that you will be able to interact long-term. You need to be able to accept your ability while still making sure that you take steps to control it so that you are not entirely overwhelmed by them.

Peace and happiness are attained by this through being able to control the way that you respond. You are learning that you may not be able to control your emotions, but you can learn to control the way that you respond to them. You can learn to take away that lack of control over the emotions that you are feeling just by making sure that you know that they do not have to rule over you.

Hobbies

Hobbies are an essential part of any person's life, no matter what they are. Do you want to make crazy fan videos of your favorite songs being played with you tapping away at random objects around you? You can do that! Do you want to create miniature models of all of your favorite foods out of clay? Great! No matter what your hobbies are, if they bring you that happiness that you want or need, that is enough for you.

There is no rule that hobbies have to be useful—but they should bring you joy. If they do not bring you joy, then they are probably not a hobby by definition. You need to make sure that you have areas of your life that you enjoy. Yes, being an adult can be dull sometimes, especially if you find that your job is draining. However, you need to figure out ways that you can allow yourself to enjoy yourself.

What is it that matters the most to you? Do you enjoy making music? Do you like to write? Even if you happen to have been fortunate enough to turn your hobby into your career, you still need time to work on projects for yourself as well. You must be able to find that time for yourself so that you can be happy as well.

Self-Compassion

Finally, every empath alive needs self-compassion. It is, so hardtop be kind to oneself when you feel like you are at fault for everything that has happened. You need to learn how you can be kind to yourself. Whether you like it or not, you are an empath for life. There is no way that you can completely erase those tendencies—you need to be able to be kind to yourself for it. The sooner that you can accept what it is that you are as an empath, the sooner you can be kinder to yourself.

Self-compassion also requires you to be kind to yourself in other ways as well. Make sure that you are regularly taking care of what you need when you need it. If you know that you are tired, take a mental health break. Take the time that you will need to stop and unwind. Figure out ways that you are able to meet your needs. Forgive yourself when you make mistakes.

Empaths are already highly sensitive by nature. There is no reason that you should make it worse because you are upset with yourself. Take the time to forgive yourself and love yourself. The self-compassion will take you far in life if you want to be truly happy.

Chapter 6: Virtues in Stoicism

The Stoics of ancient Greece recognized four key virtues within their philosophy. They focused on what they referred to as prudence, justice, fortitude, and temperance. These four virtues were believed to be the goals of the philosophical ethics of the time. These four virtues defined what we all ought to work toward if we want to be happy in life. Stoicism was no exception—they looked toward these four virtues to guide them.

These four virtues will guide everything that you do in life if you were to live the Stoic lifestyle. To be a Stoic, you must make these virtues the key to everything that you do. They ought to guide you through every aspect of your life so that you know what you are doing. They should drive you forward, to keep you actively striving to achieve that happiness—Eudaimonia in the Greek understanding of ethics.

Within this chapter, we are going to take a closer look at the history of the Stoics and their teachings, understanding the points that they were trying to make when they did to get that better understanding of what it means to live the Stoic life. We are going to take a look at the role of virtue in ethics before finally addressing the four virtues that were believed to be the guiding forces in ancient Greek ethics.

A Closer Look at Stoicism

Before we begin, stop, and consider one point: Stoicism is not simply a way of thinking or a type of knowledge. Rather, philosophy, with Stoicism included, is a lifestyle. It is a way to live—it is exercises and practicing a specific type of life because you believe that it is the right one without any room for disagreement. Usually, philosophies of all kinds have their own justifications for why they matter and why they ought to be regarded as the right one. For Stoicism, we have the virtues justifying and validating its existence.

Stoicism is believed to begin in Plato's *Sophist,* in which he asks for some sort of indication for what is real in life, or what is existing in the moment. One of the answers that is considered is that being able to act or be acted upon is what marks us as being existent. Essentially, that which is is anything that can be acted upon or can act itself.

For the Stoics, this was accepted—however, they added to it. In the Stoic perspective, only bodies exist. Bodies can act or be acted upon, and therefore, they exist. They disregard the idea of materialists or spiritualists, instead choosing to specify that all that exists is the physical body itself. However, despite the fact that that which is, is limited specifically to the physical body, they recognize that there is also room for spirit as well. That spirit, however, is created as energy, so to speak—it is the combination of the elements—fire, air, water, and earth. The active elements, in particular, fire and air, can create the pneuma—the spirit. The pneuma is believed to sustain the body and growth. Pneuma is what keeps us rooted, keeps us what we are physically. Of course, this is just barely breaching the surface of Stoicism and the arguments behind it.

Stoicism, as we know it today, comes from some of the followers of this philosophy. In particular, Marcus Aurelius became one of the greatest proponents of this type of thinking—he showed that he could possess the virtues that we will be discussing shortly and used those virtues to rule better than any other, according to historians.

Marcus Aurelius is commonly referred to as the last of the Five Good Emperors during the time in which the Roman Empire was ruled through wisdom and virtue—and we get a glimpse into his virtue through reading his *Meditations*. Stoicism became his way of life. The stony exterior, the stolid nonreactive traits, helped him to thrive as an emperor. It helped him to deal with stress as it inundated him, and he was able to rule one of the most influential, powerful nations that the world has ever seen.

The Virtues

Virtue is defined as being of the best disposition—it is a state in which someone is acting in ways interpreted to be good or true—they are observing the laws justly and ensuring that the individual is living as well as he or she can. Virtue is difficult to define—and the definition will vary greatly from person to person, from dictionary to dictionary, and from culture to culture. However, one thing holds true, no matter what—virtues are desirable. They are those traits that we ought to strive toward. They are the traits that aid us in figuring out what it is that society values from us so that we can be good and true. To be virtuous is to be just; it is to be adherent to those values that matter the most.

In Stoicism, the end goal from living the virtuous life is to achieve Eudaimonia—a state in which you can achieve utter happiness or fulfillment. It is the good that is created of all goods—the ability to live well and to be perfect in regard to virtue. Effectively, it is being able to live a good, true life with regard to the world around you, to be willing and able to follow the rules and considerations of the world that are the most important of all.

The virtues were seen as a way to control their passions. Passions ought to be avoided—fear, lust, distress, and delight ought to be feelings that are avoided. They cloud the mind; they prevent you from making decisions that matter the most, and because of that, it is important to avoid the passions. Passion, while acceptable today as something that is laudable is something that ought to be avoided, according to the Stoics. If life is all about living virtuously, passion is the greatest threat to exactly that. The virtues are the antidote to passion—they will allow for the individuals to live the virtuous, happy, rational life that they wish to lead all by clearing out those passions and preventing them from taking control.

Within Stoicism, it is believed that passion cannot enter the mind without the permission of the individual. Reason is what invites passion in, and is also what clears it out. Reason, then, becomes one's own worst enemy if it is not truly forged into what it ought to be, and that is where the rational, virtuous life comes into play. The virtues of life can teach the individual to fight back those traits. It can teach the individual to hold back those passions and prevent them from taking a stronghold over the individual's life, allowing them to effectively create the life that they want to live. Effectively, passion will be prevented through honing rationality through the use of virtues.

In terms of Stoicism itself, there are four key cardinal virtues that matter the most. These four virtues will guide the Stoic through life accordingly, teaching him or her everything that they need to know if they want to thrive. Let's take some time to get to know each of these key virtues.

Prudence or wisdom

The first that we will look at is wisdom or prudence—you will see it translated as either of these two words. It is the ability by which human happiness can be produced. It is the knowledge of good and bad, the knowledge that will help you to achieve happiness because of that knowledge. It will help us judge that which must be done and which we must not. Prudence, then, is the idea of moral wisdom—it is the most important of the virtues.

When living by wisdom or prudence, you must make sure that you are living a life with a full grasp of the situation. You understand that ultimately, the way that you interact with the world is dependent upon the ways in which you engage with those around you. It is dependent upon what is good or bad in life. You need to understand right and wrong, and that is done through prudence.

It is to understand the value of logic and reason. You choose the right thing to do, no matter how difficult it is for you because it is simply the right thing to do. It is this concept that you will not be attempting to make decisions based on emotions, but based on what makes the most sense at any given time. To live with prudence is to live with reason and logic, making it one of the most compelling of the points that are pushed within Stoicism.

It also refers to our ability to judge or weigh the value of things in the world rationally—with indifference. It is essential to being able to respond to the world around us in accordance with their values. If something is upsetting to you, for example, but is not actually important, all things considered, you must be able to let it go. This will help you to identify what matters the most and what you should be acting upon.

Justice or morality

Next comes the idea of justice or morality. Keep in mind that the translation to justice is a bit narrower than what is believed to be intended by the original Stoics—to refer to justice is so much more than just legal. It encompasses moral justice, as well. Justice refers to the unanimity of the soul itself—recognizing the discipline of the parts of the soul to create a law-abiding individual, an individual who treats their peers with value and justice. It is to obey the laws, but also to obey what matters morally speaking as well.

It is to treat people with fairness and kindness, along with that idea of justice; it is meant in the sense of social virtue rather than strictly legal. Marcus Aurelius states that justice is the most important of the virtues, recognizing that without justice, without that feeling of kindness or camaraderie with those around you, you can never truly interact appropriately or accordingly with those around you and the world itself as a society will struggle, or even fail.

Justice is the idea that moral wisdom is applied to the actions that we perform—it takes that understanding of what is and is not right and then applies that to action. It is to act with wisdom, effectively, to ensure that you are treating the people around you fairly. It is to approach the world with impartiality, meaning that you do not give anyone any preferential treatment in how you engage with them, and through kindness or courtesy.

Temperance or moderation

Next, we take a look at moderation or temperance. This is being able to regulate one's own reactions to the world around you; it is to be able to recognize that there is a line between wants and needs and that we must be able to control that line, to tow it, and to not give in hedonistically. It is wrong, according to the Stoics, for us to give in to something simply because we want it. Effectively, we ought to deny ourselves that which we do not rationally need—it is admirable to give yourself what you need but not to be ruled by your pleasures and what you may want, even if you cannot quite have it.

Think of temperance as mindfulness—it is being able to be self-aware so that you do not let your emotions get the best of you. You ought to be self-disciplined enough, for example, to prevent yourself from acting in ways that will be pleasant now but will not be good for you in the future. Effectively, you ought to be conscious of what you need and what you can avoid. Impulses, the desire to give in to certain wants, ought to be withheld. In Stoicism, moderation is pushed and defined as good self-discipline.

This is where that detached nature of the Stoic comes into play—when you are stoic, you are able to get that objective representation—that ability to deny yourself any desire or fear that may otherwise cloud your judgment. You are able to figure out what it is that you need to do through an objective lens, meaning that you will be able to make a better judgment over the whole situation.

Think about it—when you are emotional, are you thinking clearly? Despite the fact that so many of us would assert that yes, even in emotional states, they are thinking clearly, this is not actually the case. Remember, emotions are there to influence the way that you behave. They are influential by nature—that influence means that you are not going to be thinking clearly or rationally; you are guided by the emotions that you are feeling.

In Stoicism, however, the obvious answer is to let go of those emotions, stopping them from being able to entirely influence the individual in ways that are less than savory. If you want to be able to make those clear, dispassionate judgments, you must be able to achieve that freedom from unhealthy passions that will otherwise cloud your mind.

Fortitude or courage

Finally, the last virtue is fortitude or courage. This is being unmovable. To be courageous is to be able to behave without fear guiding you. It is to have that strict confidence in yourself—the knowledge that you have all of the facts and that you can use them. It is being restrained, about recognizing that you can withhold that fear that you may have facing something. It is being able to stand face to face with a terrible threat, something that is horrifying, and remain clear thinking in the moment. It is being able to balance out that fear and sense of danger with a sense of calmness—of being able to protect the soul, to ensure that you are feeling confident enough to take on anything that comes your way.

To have fortitude is to be calm. It is to be rational. It is to be able to persevere, even when all looks bleak. It is effectively to be courageous—but it goes a step further with Stoicism. Beyond just being courageous, Stoicism also recognizes that it is imperative to also be able to fight back—to be able to recognize that pain and discomfort must be endured as well. Through being fortitudinous, you are able to endure, and through endurance, you are able to keep a clearer mind, so that you are able to master yourself and the passions that you have.

Effectively, those who are courageous or fortitudinous are able to endure—they are able to conquer their fears or pains that they are suffering from. They are able to see the ways that they must interact, to recognize that at the end of the day, they must maintain control. It is only then that they are able to achieve the success that they want or need. When you are able to endure, you are able to renounce that control that pain or fear would have over you.

Of course, to be fortitudinous requires that there is that fear somewhere. You cannot conquer and deny your fear if there is no fear to conquer or deny. This is paradoxical, and yet, perfect by design. To be able to be virtuous, you must be able to recognize moderation in the first place. To have the virtues, you must also have the vices to defeat. Stoicism is not seeking the abolishment of those vices; rather, it is seeking to overcome them despite their presence to become a better individual; to become someone that is able to be virtuous in nature.

Chapter 7: The Stoic Life Is the Good Life

The Stoic life is one of simplicity; it is to be able to live your life on reason rather than going through life as an animal, allowing your impulses and feelings to drive you. Think about it—humankind has been given a gift, whether by design or by evolution. We are able to think rationally. We can overcome the temptation to engage with the world around us entirely emotionally. We can hold ourselves back when we feel that temptation to act passionately. When you can prevent yourself from those behaviors that are harmful, you know that you are able to live a life in which you are able to be true to the virtues that Stoicism advocates for.

When it comes to living a Stoic life, you are able to live a life of quiet simplicity; you are not complicating your life with emotions or irrationality. You are able to live a life that will help toward ensuring that you are constantly attempting to become your best self. You will constantly work to strive for what really matters the most—a life in which you are able to do everything that it is that matters to you.

Of course, to live the Stoic life is not always easy. It takes time to live the Stoic life, to truly reject the passions in favor of the virtues. It is difficult to let go of those emotions that control you and prevent you from working the way that you should be. It is difficult to figure out how you should and should not engage with the world, but in this chapter, you will see what needs to be done to live that life. If you want a good, simple life, you must follow these steps. To be Stoic is to practice changing your life; it is to recognize that you can always do better, that you can always find new perspectives to follow, and that you are able to defeat your passions so that you can become someone better. You can reject the childish attitudes that you may be embodying by learning to better yourself, and in doing so, you bring yourself closer to success than ever.

Control the Thinking

To begin with your Stoic training, you must recognize that you need control. According to Epictetus, one of the original Stoics, you must make sure that you are in control of what you can be. Ultimately, according to Epictetus, you cannot control very much in the world. You have no sway over the people around you, for example—you can influence them, but influence is not the same as genuine control. They are not something that you can force into behaving a certain way on a whim in the sense that you can control your foot and make it move. You cannot control the world around you entirely. You cannot even totally control yourself—you cannot choose when you will get sick or when you will be injured, for example. So, then, what can you control, you may ask?

You can control your thoughts. The one thing in this great big world that you can control is your thoughts. This is imperative to remember—when you control your thoughts, you control the way that you engage with the world around you. Thoughts will influence feelings and feelings will influence behaviors, and the sooner that you develop an understanding and an affinity for this fact, the sooner that you can ensure that you live the Stoic life that you have always wanted to set out and enjoy. Think about it this way—when you think positively, you feel positive. When you feel positive, you tend to behave positively, as well.

Because you can control your thoughts on a whim, you can effectively make sure that no matter what, you are in the right mindset. This means that you can reject the negative emotions that will try to control you. You can remind yourself that you are not behaving logically if such a time were to arise. You can make sure that you are regulating yourself so that you can trust that you are making the right decisions. If you can do that, you can control yourself.

Try this for a week: Every single time that you have a negative thought, remind yourself that you ought to be thinking positively—and enforce it.

Keep in mind that this does not mean that you should reject any emotionality that you have—emotions are there for a reason! They are like warning flags, letting us know what is going on around us. However, you should also make sure that if something is happening around you, you are able to override those negative emotions. You can prevent them from being able to control you or make you do something that you are going to reject.

Emotions are ultimately the product of the judgments that we make—if you realize that the judgments that you are making are actually becoming problematic for you for some reason, you can reject the idea entirely. You can redirect and correct yourself so that you can protect yourself. If you can do this, you can make sure that ultimately, you are able to make the right judgments that ultimately will matter more than anything else. You can be happy if you can alter those judgments. Stoicism is paradoxical in the sense that you have control over next to nothing, and yet you have unlimited control over the happiness that you can attain.

Train the Mind

Next, if you want to live the Stoic life, you must train your mind as much as you can. This means that you must work to understand the world around you. You must think differently if you can. You must make sure that you consider the positions of other people as well. If you think differently, you can start to see perspectives that you may not have realized the first time around. You may wonder whether or not the behaviors that you complete actually matter. They do, in fact—you can acknowledge other perspectives, and in doing so, you can ensure that you are learning more.

Stoics work to train their minds—they stop and look at the world and the life that they lived for the day. They consider whether or not there was anything that ultimately was not particularly important that led to annoyance or irritation, and if there was something, how that can be avoided in the future. This process of constant self-reflection allows for the Stoics to constantly be training their minds, shielding themselves against the negativity that they may otherwise face. When this is done properly, it aids in making sure that you are making better decisions every day.

It is impossible for any of us to be perfect—there is no way that you will ever get every last moment of your life just right. However, what you can learn to do is figure out what it is that you did wrong today so that tomorrow, you can do better. The sooner that you embrace this, the sooner that you can succeed.

You can also start each and every day that you will almost definitely encounter people that you will dislike throughout the day. Someone will do something that is going to frustrate you. Someone will seem ungrateful. You will find that ultimately, you will be unhappy at some point—but you can learn to control it. You can learn to choose happiness. You can learn to reflect that most of those people that you will encounter are not inherently frustrated at you—rather, they are probably unintentionally upset, a slave to their own passions and judgments. You can choose not to add to that by refusing to be moved by them.

Practice Acceptance

Similarly to being able to practice training the mind, you can make sure that you are able to accept that things are what they are. One important fact to keep in mind is that the world is not circling around you. The world does not care about you. The world does not care that ultimately, you are behaving a certain way—most people probably do not even know who you are anyway. However, when you accept that your position in the world is one of unimportance, you can start to accept that the context of what you do is inconsequential. The universe is not going to give you what you want just because you want it—because you *are* inconsequential. You can embrace what the universe does give you, however.

To practice acceptance is to recognize that while you cannot control what happens around you, you can accept it and then control the way that you respond. When you are able to control the way that you engage with the world, you can find that ultimately, you become the gatekeeper to your own happiness. You cannot get upset over something going wrong when you simply accept that things are what they are, and there is little that you can do about it.

By changing your attitude instead of trying to fight against something that you have no control over, you can ensure that you are in control. Despite the paradox, this is the perfect way for you to maintain that happiness that you need if you want to thrive as a Stoic.

Practice Minimalism

Another key practice of Stoicism is to relinquish the idea that you must have everything to be happy. According to Epictetus, *"Wealth consists not in having great possessions, but in having few wants."* Effectively, you are not wealthy if you have everything around you but still want more—than the desire for more and more materialistic goods is only going to drag you down further. It is only going to make it harder for you to achieve that true happiness that you were looking for. Rather than allowing yourself to be eaten up by that materialistic nonsense, Stoicism encourages the renouncement of needing constant materialistic justifications.

Instead of constantly seeking out more and more items around you, you should be paying closer attention to what you have. You do not need the latest and greatest iPhone to be happy. You do not need $1,000,000 in the bank to be happy. What you need, however, is the people in your life that you love.

Remember, Stoicism is not about renouncing emotions—it is about renouncing being enslaved by them. You are allowed to love people in Stoicism. You are allowed to find that there are people that you care deeply about. They are who matter in your life. Being able to strive toward happiness requires you to want less—it requires you to find that happiness through being satisfied with what you have.

Practice Gratitude

Of course, being able to be satisfied with what you have requires you to practice gratitude. When you are grateful for the world that you live in and the people in it, you are able to be happier. This also helps you stop yourself from constantly seeking to get more around you. Life is not about dreaming of having what you currently lack—it is about being able to see that you should be thankful for what you have.

Think about it for a moment, if the people that you loved the most in life were suddenly to disappear, what would you do? How would you feel if suddenly, you were without your best friend? Your children? Your spouse or significant other? You would probably be devastated to lose them—but do you appreciate them in the moment?

We take for granted the people around us all too often. We assume that they will be there regardless of what happens, and that could not be further from the truth. The truth of the matter is that we treat everyone as if they are given rather than a luxury. We have the luxury of knowing those people around us. We have the luxury of having our friends, family, and children. They are a blessing—and it is difficult for many people to accept this. We take what we have for granted.

Every now and then, practice imagining what you would do if you suddenly found yourself without. Walk to work instead of driving. Leave your phone at home for a day. Spend a day not engaging with those that you love. It is an exercise in seeing what you have. Ultimately, we oftentimes find that we do not miss what we have until it is gone.

However, as a Stoic, you owe it to yourself to recognize what you have. You owe it to yourself to recognize the truth of the matter—that what you have matters immensely and that what you have ought to be honored and cherished even though you have it.

Be Kind and Cheerful

Remember, one of the virtues was to be just to people around you—you ought to treat people fairly and kindly. The idea of justice was more along the lines of treating people kindly and fairly, a sort of social virtue. It is important for you to be kind to those around you. It is imperative to recognize that happiness that we have comes from human experience.

The greatest joys that we have of all are our inner joys—those that we can delight in within ourselves without having to purchase something or do something that encourages those feelings. It is imperative to recognize this; to live by the idea that at the end of the day, we must be kind to ourselves, and also to those around us.

By being kind to those around you, you are providing other people with the goodness from your hearts. Goodness spread throughout the world is what will help the world continue to progress. Your goodness into the world will help you to advance society, and that is fulfilling on its own. Even better, it costs you nothing to be kind to those around you.

Practice What You Preach

Finally, remember that at the end of the day, living what you say is important to you is the best thing that you can do. It is not enough to simply voice that you believe something—you must also live it. Think about it—you could say that you are all for banning plastic bottles as you sip at a plastic water bottle. Is that really something that you care about if you are voicing that you want to do so as you are sitting there, using one?

To practice what you preach shows conviction; it shows that you actually do care about what you are saying. You must make sure that you always do this—you must practice what you preach so that people show that you are serious. When you do not, you come across as pretentious, or like you are only saying something because you want the credit for something that you honestly do not care about. It is not enough for you to voice something. You must act, and Stoicism regularly pushes for this.

In Stoicism, you are obligated to act in ways that are going to be true to your own personal philosophies, no matter what they are. When you are practicing Stoicism, it is expected of you to ask yourself how you can act in any given moment and if that particular choice is really the right one for you, given the context. When you are able to live the right kind of life with the right kinds of decisions, you can usually show everyone around you that you are, in fact, dedicated to the morals and values that you have been advocating for.

Ultimately, then, Stoicism as a practice is meant to be something that you can use to control the way that you engage with the world around you. It is meant to guide you to better your life. It is to work to better yourself, to ensure that you live a life that matters to you. When you can do that, when you can make sure that the life that you live is one that matters the most to you, you can ensure that the life that you live is one that is valuable.

You owe it to yourself to better yourself. You owe it to yourself to make sure that you do not allow yourself to get entirely caught up in materialism. You must make sure that you always try to engage with other people in the best ways possible. You ought to make sure that what you do is going to aid in bettering the world. To live the good Stoic life is to live the life in which you do not let the world around you that is out of your control overwhelm you. It is imperative that the life that you live is one that you will be able to control everything. If there is one takeaway on what the proper Stoic life is, it is that you have control over the way that you react and when you can acknowledge that, you can get far.

Chapter 8: Stoicism and Emotions

Though it is used otherwise often in writing, Stoicism is not to be emotionless. Make sure that you get that thought out of your mind. To be Stoic is not to be emotionless—it is to be nonreactive. However, the two are not the same thing, despite the fact that many people would believe otherwise. Stoicism is not about repressing emotions. It is about feeling. It is about striving for Eudaimonia—for that joy in life in which you are able to control yourself and your reactions. The sooner that you can achieve that state of Eudaimonia, the happier you will be.

This means that Stoics, then, are emotional by nature. Of course, they are—they are people just like anyone else, and people are living, emotional beings. People seem to think of them as unemotional, but in reality, to be a Stoic is to be constantly striving to be the best human that you can be—emotions and all. This means that you have no choice but to accept those emotions for what they are. You have to make sure that you are embracing those emotions, that you are embracing the idea of who you are and what you want. The sooner that you can embrace humanity, the sooner that you can get on the right track.

To be Stoic is to live according to nature. This challenges the Stoics; it encourages us to constantly figure out what our place in the universe is. What are we? How do we exist? Are we real? Are we able to prove that we are real? What does it matter if we are? These are questions that matter to the Stoic—it becomes imperative to recognize that ultimately, the way that you engage with the world around you is important, and that is done through emotions.

Of course, the approach to emotional life for the Stoics is a bit different than most would consider. Rather than being in touch with all emotions and letting them run rampant, Stoics look to control themselves. They approach their emotions as being just that—impulsive feelings. They are like the weather, so to speak; rather than something that ought to be treated as reliable or dependable, or even predictable, they should be seen as natural occurrences that will cause us to make changes to our behavior.

Think about it—you change your behavior based on the weather. You may wear different clothes. You may wear sunglasses if the sun is shining or if it has snowed and created a massive amount of glare. If it is hot out and sunny, you will probably put on sunscreen. If the roads are icy, you will probably slow down. Your emotions are much like these storms—they will constantly influence your mind and your actions, and that is what the Stoics tend to address.

The Stoics see that your emotions are highly volatile. They see that it is possible for your emotions to rule you and to try to drag you into behaving in certain ways that may not be appropriate—and they then decide to control it. Rather than giving in to those behaviors, the Stoics learn to weather the storm—they learn what they can do to prevent those emotions from taking control over the whole situation. They prevent themselves from being able to be flooded by those emotions that will otherwise cause them to behave to other people in negative manners.

Ultimately, emotions matter to the Stoic. They become guiding factors in just about every point of the Stoic's life, and because of that, it becomes imperative to judge accordingly. You must make sure that you are engaging with the world around you as well as you can, and that means being able to control the emotions that you are putting out, or at the very least, controlling the reactions to the emotions that you have.

There are ultimately three positive emotions that are identified by the Stoics and three negative ones as well. These emotions guide just about everything in life, according to

Stoics. You have the good emotions of joy, wish, and caution, along with the three passions, the negative emotions of pleasure, appetite or lust, and fear. Of course, if you are unfamiliar with Stoicism, you are probably scratching your head right now, trying to figure out the difference between the two. It is slight, but it is there, and the sooner that you learn the differences, the sooner that you can understand the emotional states of the Stoic.

When you recognize the differences between the two, you start to see those small subtleties that matter—the technicalities upon which the two are so similar, and yet able to be entirely separated out from each other. When it comes right down to it, the most important thing to remember is that there is a good and a bad emotion for everything.

Keep in mind that these emotions that you are being given will encompass all others as well. These are the overarching categories on either side, and everything else will sort of funnel into one of the six given.

The Stoics and Joy Versus Pleasure

First comes joy versus pleasure. Joy and pleasure are not inherently the same, despite what many people would think. In Stoicism, there is an emphasis on finding joy rather than the passion of pleasure. When you recognize the difference between the two, you will start to understand what matters more.

Joy is happiness that is not dependent upon what happens. No matter what happens in that situation, you will still have joy. Think about it this way—have you ever heard the expression that a bad pizza is still good? Sure, a bad pizza is probably going to be disappointing if you thought that you were in the market for something better. However, most of the time, even a bad pizza, so long as it is not burnt or rotten with normal toppings on it, is going to still be good. It is hard to mess up pizza, and you will probably still enjoy it to some degree or another.

Pleasure, however, is dependent upon the outcome. It is dependent upon what may come next to make things happen. Pleasure happens when you enjoy what the end result is. You may find pleasure in, for example, winning some money on your scratch ticket. If asked if you find that gambling with scratch tickets is pleasurable, you may say yes—but the answer is that it is really only pleasurable when you win. Otherwise, it is frustrating and honestly feels like a waste of money. When you recognize this difference, you start to see the truth—joy is virtuous and pure. Pleasure is hedonistic.

Hedonists are seen as the opposite of Stoics oftentimes—in hedonism, the idea is that pleasure is deemed the highest form of good that exists. It is important to maximize pleasure, to enjoy what is happening as much as possible to ensure that you are happy. To be good is to be pleasurable. However, in Stoicism, that emotionality and that cling to pleasure are actually seen as problematic. It is not pleasure that is desired, argue the Stoics, but rather, the joy that they get through doing the right thing.

Think for a moment, then, about what makes something enjoyable—many people will say that it feels good or it seems like the right thing to do. To feel joy is to feel morally sound. It is to feel as if you are being true to the virtues that you value. When you are able to be joyous about something, you recognize that you are happy no matter what happens—you have made the right moral decision because of that.

The Stoics and Wish Versus Lust

Next comes the idea of wish versus lust or appetite. This particular dichotomy may seem strange as well—after all is a wish, not some degree of lust, or is lust, not a wish? However, there is an important distinguishing factor here—pining for things that you do not have, lusting over something that you cannot get, is greedy. If you are lusting over something, you are acting with greed.

Think about it—if you are sitting there, looking at an attractive person, wishing that you could have your way with them, are you thinking in a Stoic manner? You are being lustful in the literal sense of the word—you want something selfishly without regard for what the end result will be. If you decided to pursue the other person, even after the other person expressed being uninterested, you would be chasing after something irrationally in hopes of getting something good.

However, lust is taken one step further in Stoicism—you do not just lust after someone that you find attractive. Rather, you lust over anything that you want but cannot have, or that you do not have. It is that desire and waste of energy toward something that you hope to get despite knowing that it is unlikely Greed becomes that appetite, that lust, for material things. Of course, you can also lust after other things as well, such as lusting after revenge for something that has happened. If you are able to recognize that lust is something negative or problematic, you recognize that ultimately, no matter what happens, you are working against yourself. You are hurting yourself—you are wasting energy.

Wish, then, is a feeling of, "Wow, I really wish I had this thing, but I know that I do not need that to experience joy." You are allowed to want things—there are no rules against not wanting to get the newest phone after your old one shattered when you dropped it. You are welcome to get new things that you want—but remember that ultimately, those things that you want are not going to determine your happiness. They will not bring you joy for the sake of having them—or rather, you will not feel an absence of joy if you do not get the item in the first place. When it comes right down to it, the emotions that you feel, the behaviors that you have, and more, are all based on whether you are acting in lust or in wish. You can wish for anything that you want, so long as you can make the distinction between wanting and needing something for your happiness.

The Stoics and Caution Versus Fear

Finally comes the idea of caution versus fear. Again, these may seem quite similar at first glance—is it not a bit pedantic to state that fear and caution are not the same? After all, whether you are cautious or afraid, you are going to be taking the same steps to avoid whatever it is that you believe is dangerous in that situation. It is important for you to recognize the truth—that there is some sort of defining difference between the two.

Remember that to feel fear does not make you weak. It does not mean that you are wrong—and there are some situations in which fear is entirely justifiable. However, you should also remember that ultimately, the way that you feel is something that you can influence.

Fear is defined as an irrational aversion. You expect that there is going to be some sort of danger, and you act accordingly. You believe that the threat will happen, and you start to plan. Of course, this comes at a major cost. Instead of being happy in the moment, you find that you are actually incredibly unhappy instead. You struggle to interact with the ways that you should be encouraged to behave. You struggle to act in ways that are going to be rational. You tell yourself that you are afraid that something will happen, so you have to take certain precautions.

Imagine this—you are suddenly convinced that you are due for a major earthquake in your area that is going to cause utter destruction across the population. You tell yourself that the earthquake is going to be so bad that food lines and other sorts of trade routes, which we need to survive, will be shattered, so you decide to stock up to the best of your ability to prevent yourself from being unprepared. You are terrified that the earthquake may come, and you do everything in your power to prepare, followed by living your life terrified that things are going to get worse. You keep yourself at home. You lock yourself away and refuse to go anywhere. You spend your day hiding under your desk, believing that at the very least, you will be safe under there if your roof collapses. This is fear.

In this example, you are afraid of something that may come at some point. You let go of your current joy that you could have in favor of letting the future potential negativity take it away. When it comes right down to it, the way that you engage with the world is entirely dependent upon the way that you view those concerns that you have.

On the other hand, if you behave with caution, you recognize that sometimes, life does something unpredictable or something that is going to be uncomfortable. However, instead of living underneath a desk and refusing to go out, you decide that you are going to prepare as much as you can. You make sure that everything that is important to you is sealed up. Furniture is secured to the walls so that it will not tip over in an earthquake. You make sure that any items that matter to you are secured so that they will not be destroyed. You work hard to ensure that everything is as safe as possible, knowing that in doing so, you can protect yourself as much as possible. However, you refuse to change your life for a maybe. You refuse to sacrifice your current joy for potential dangers. The earthquake could be in 10 minutes or ten centuries—but you should be prepared anyway. In being cautious, you are able to approach with awareness. You understand that ultimately, it is important to plan accordingly and ensure that you are taking care of everything to the best of your ability.

Chapter 9: Finding Inner Peace

Peace of mind is the ultimate goal for most people. It is so great to find that peaceful point—that point in which you are certain that you have done everything that you can and attempted to live the right life for yourself. That point in which you are able to accept that you are living your best life and enjoying it. Think of the lucky few who have achieved this—they are calm. They are patient. They are able to deal with just about anything with kindness. Despite just how easy these people make it seem, these people must work hard to make this sort of emotional state occur.

To be at peace is highly demanding on the mind, contrary to popular belief. To be at peace requires you to be able to develop enough emotional control to not give in whenever something goes wrong. To be at peace is to ensure that you are able to succeed accordingly. It is to recognize that ultimately, the ways that you behave in life are dependent upon your mindset.

If you want to be at peace, Stoicism is for you. Stoic philosophers have been pursuing that degree of peace for centuries. Marcus Aurelius dedicated every morning to working with his journals. Epictetus constantly stated that men are disturbed by the thoughts that are developed rather than what happens around you. It is important for people to remember that ultimately, to be at peace is to be in control of the mind. It is to be in control of the thoughts. Stoicism has endured for thousands of years and is still so popular because it allows for that degree of control that people want. It teaches people how they can begin to control themselves. It reminds them of what they need to do so that they can guide themselves throughout their own lives on the right paths. If you are able to develop that ability to behave Stoically, you can live a peaceful life.

Both Marcus Aurelius and Epictetus saw philosophy not as something to use every now and then, but as a way of life—they constantly revisited the philosophies they were studying. They regarded the philosophy of Stoicism as something that could be used to aid them in just about every aspect of life. They learned to become more reflective and less reactive. They turned inward instead of outward. They learned to keep their cool, to recognize that sometimes, the best thing that you can do in life is to simply let things go and move on.

When it comes right down to it, to be peaceful, to live your most successful, happiest life, you must embrace these concepts. You must let go of the idea that ultimately, you are stuck with your negativity or in the mindset that you are in. If you want to achieve inner peace yourself, there are steps that you can take to ensure that you make it happen. It may not be easy, but it is something that you can do for yourself. All you have to do is set out to make it happen. Within this chapter, we are going to look at the several steps toward finding inner peace as a Stoic. Live these ideas. Let them guide you and the life that you live. You will discover what matters the most in your life, and you will discover that you are all the happier for it.

Let Go of Anxiety

It is so easy to get caught up in the idea that things are far worse than they may seem, and the unfortunate reality is that as soon as you do that, you find yourself in a constant spiral in which you want to do better, but you cannot. You get yourself stuck in this mindset of being unable to manage the current situation that you are in because you are too busy catastrophizing to realize that things are not actually that bad in the first place.

We tend to be more afraid of all of the what-ifs rather than the realities of situations, and because of that, it becomes important to let go of them. Yes, this is easier said than done, but it is highly powerful. If you want to escape the anxiety that you have and live a Stoic life, you must be making it a point to engage with your life in the most beneficial way that you can muster. You must make sure that you work to provide yourself with everything that you know to be true. You must work to ensure that you are able to remind yourself that catastrophizing never helped anyone.

Remind yourself to stay in the moment—practice mindfulness. Refuse to allow your emotions that you are feeling rule the moment. Let yourself focus on the world around you in the moment and keep yourself there. Are things actually that bad? When you stop feeling so anxious all of the time, you can usually work to feel better and do better. If you want to feel at peace, you must make sure that you reject the idea of anxiety. Let yourself be who you are and let yourself only focus on the present problems.

Accept Mortality

It is so easy to get caught up in the idea of your impending death to the point that you tend to forget the truth of the matter—we all die at some point, and we will never know when that is. Ultimately, the only people that know when their death is, are those that are about to end them—at which point, they have already accepted their own mortality.

However, dwelling about your death, when it will happen, and what you can do to mitigate the death that will happen eventually will only cause you to miss out on what is happening in the moment. Instead of enjoying whatever is left of your life, you are finding yourself constantly worrying about what could go wrong. You may not go on that cruise because you are afraid that it will be a repeat of the Titanic. You will pass up that dream job because you think the extra 20 minutes per day of freeway driving puts your life at too much risk. Rational? Not really.

When you accept that you will die at some point and that there will be nothing that you can do about it when it happens, you can begin to remove some of that anxiety over it. You will be able to recognize that death will happen at some point, and in making peace, you can then work with trying to live the right kind of life. You can work to make sure that you are motivated to live each life to its fullest, to work to the best of your ability to live the best possible life that you can so that you do not die with regrets.

Your fear of death should be shifted into a motivation to do the most with what you have—as much as you can. This means that you need to work hard with yourself. This means that you must work to constantly follow what matters to you.

You must make sure that you are engaging in the actions that matter the most to you. If that means that you are going to travel the world to volunteer time, then do it. If you are going to breed puppies, then do it. Life is short. Do not let it all pass by until you have none left to live.

Remember Whose Opinions Matter the Most

Perhaps one of the largest sources of anxiety that we have these days comes from the worry about what other people think about us. We all constantly worry about other people think about ourselves even though ultimately, we all tend to prioritize ourselves over other people. When it comes right down to it, the opinions of everyone around you are not as important as your own. When it comes right down to it, it is your opinion that matters the most, and when you recognize that and take that into consideration, you can start to erase some of those worries that you have.

Think about it—today, we are endlessly connected online. We are constantly able to get back to people quickly and easily. We are all constantly inundated with opinions, and if it is on the internet, everyone has one. However, ultimately, when it comes right down to it, the only opinion that truly matters is your own. It does not matter what your neighbor thinks about your haircut—what do you think about it?

Humans are social animals, and because we are, we worry about what other people think about us. However, in reality, there are so many different people in the world with so many different opinions and desires that if you were to try to consider every single person's opinion, you would never get anything done. Why, then, do you let the people that are in your immediate vicinity pass judgment?

Spending your life worrying about what everyone else thinks is only setting yourself up for feeling like you have to compete against others. It sets you up for the expectation of keeping up with the Joneses, and that is a huge problem—you doing so will remove just about any peace that you could have ever possibly attained all by virtue of the fact that you are now so worried about being seen as something that you may not be that you are not focusing on what matters.

Keep your focus on what matters—your own thoughts. Make sure that you live a life that makes you happy. Let go of the idea that you have to be liked by all. Instead, focus on what you can do to be kind and disciplined. What can you do to master tolerance over pain and displeasure? How can you maintain your patience? These are what matter. Ultimately, as soon as you stop caring about what everyone around you thinks, you will find that you are far happier than you thought that you would be.

Take Time to Be Still

If peace is what you want to achieve, then you have to live it as well. If you want to be truly peaceful, then you have to schedule in the time to be at peace. Even in a rapidly evolving world, where we are constantly working on more and being busier than ever, it is imperative that you take the time to ensure that you are calm and able to remind yourself that ultimately, the way that you behave matters more than anything else. If you want to be able to interact with people in a calm manner, then you have to practice calmness.

Practicing peaceful stillness is a great way for you to really embody what you want out of life. Remember, you must always practice what you preach, and this is where you start. If you want to be calm, then be physically calm. Take some time each day to spend time in peace, in stillness, and in quiet. This means that every single day, you need to prioritize some time in which you are doing nothing. No phones. No television. No talking to other people. You will sit quietly and enjoy the moment. This is all about making sure that you get to know the peace that you want.

This is something that is difficult; however—we find that ultimately, it is impossible for people to stop and really reflect in the moment. You must be able to master this art—you must be able to remind yourself that ultimately, you need calmness in your life if you want to be successful in making sure that you are keeping up with your practice. The sooner that you can practice the calmness and stillness, the sooner that your mind will learn to reflect silently and peacefully.

Find the Beauty in Every Situation

Even though Stoicism pushes this idea that you ought to be unmoving, logical, and at peace, there is still enjoyment found within it. You should always take the time that you can to find the beauty that exists. There is beauty in just about anything—you just have to know where or how to look. If you can do that, if you can figure out how to look at a situation and see the beauty in it, you can live the Stoic life with ease.

Think about it—even in a storm; there is something to look forward to. The grass and plants are getting much-needed water that they will use to provide for themselves. The animals will have new puddles that can be used to drink from. The water is pure and clean. There may be a rainbow. The sound of rain is refreshing and beautiful on its own. The smell of petrichor, that first moment in which rain starts to fall.

Beauty is visible everywhere around you. Beauty can be found in even the darkest of places, and when you realize that even those things in the world that could be painful or difficult to deal with can have some beauty in them, even if that beauty is not yet apparent to you in the moment, it can become apparent to you in the future. You can learn what it is that matters. You can learn to recognize that beauty and respect it. You can discover what it will take for you to accept what has happened so that you can respond accordingly.

The next time that you are walking somewhere stop and consider the beauty of the blue sky. Enjoy the taste of the coffee that you are sipping instead of chugging it down to get that caffeine before rushing off. Stop and savor the feeling of hot water running down your back in the shower. It will be worth it.

Imagine a New Perspective

It is so easy to get caught up in the moment when something is going wrong. It is so easy to find that you are constantly worrying about the moment that you suddenly are missing something. You can get stuck in what you see in front of you—but really, what if you consider a different perspective? What if you imagined yourself from above the problem instead of beside it?

Think about it—imagine that your car just died. You are frustrated. However, if you were to stop and imagine it from a bird's perspective, the car would probably not even be a blip on its radar. You can move further up—from an airplane; you could not even see your broken-down car. Even higher, you may not be able to see your street or even your city.

The universe is immense. When you are feeling that emotions are running high, you can remind yourself of the insignificance of the moment. Why get so worked up over something that is not really that big after all? If you want to be in a mindset of peace, this is not how you achieve it. If you are not careful, you will find that you are not able to maintain that peace at all—you are going to be stuck in the negativity of the situation. The next time that you feel that you are upset try reimagining the situation. If you were to look at things from the top down, how significant would it be?

Follow Your Code

Stoicism creates a framework that we can live by—it is a list of guidelines that we can use to reflect upon the world and determine how we align ourselves with it. If you look at the way that you engage with the world through the lens of code, you remind yourself that ultimately, you have set behaviors that you want to follow. The code becomes a sort of way for you to determine what is good and what is bad.

This helps you to achieve that inner peace as a Stoic for one reason: It simplifies things. When you approach the situation as a Stoic, you know that you are working to avoid letting emotionality play a role in your decisions. You are looking at things as rationally and logically as you can because you hope that in doing so, you can make sure that you make the right choices. Rationality becomes your code, and that brings you peace. When you know your place and what is expected of you, it is easy to be in that position or state of peace, and you will not have to do much more to maintain it. Simply make sure that you are following your code and not violating it. If it is wrong, do not do it. Stand by your convictions. Follow your moral code of conduct. If you can do this, you will be at peace with yourself.

Reflect

Finally, if you wish to achieve inner peace, the most important of all is to reflect. Make sure that you reflect upon your days every single day. In particular, Stoics tend to prefer the art of journaling. It works well to allow you to gather your thoughts, to address why you did what you did. It allows you to think about how you can better yourself in the future, or what you can do if you want to change the interactions that you have with those in your area. Though you can ultimately reflect in any way that you want to, to reflect through journaling gives you a wonderful way through which you can make sure that you are documenting all of the details. This will ensure that you know that you did something a certain way and what the implications are.

To reflect is to observe. To reflect on what matters the most in your life, you are able to focus where it matters—on the ways that you should be interacting with people. On how you can stay true to yourself. You are able to reason with yourself so that you can continue to better yourself. Every single day, you will become more and more aware of yourself and your habits, and through becoming more aware, you will find that ultimately, you have made some major moves toward being the successful Stoic that you want to be. Remember, you are always a work in progress, and through journaling, you will bring yourself closer to that feeling of peace.

Chapter 10: Tips and Strategies on Finding the Right Balance Between Stoicism and Empathic Ways of Life

Stoicism and empathic ways of life are not directly separated from each other. There is no reason that a stoic cannot be empathic, or an empath cannot be stoic. In fact, combining the two together can actually help to create a much more level mindset that can aid both. Despite the fact that empaths are highly emotional and Stoics strive to be as emotionally in control as possible, they work well together—to learn to master both types of life is to ensure that you can live a life much more likely to be successful. If you want to be able to sort of find that middle ground, following that state of both empathy and stoicism is the perfect way to ensure that you are working with the people around you in ways that you know are going to benefit everyone involved.

It is not enough to simply admit one way or another that you are stoic or empathic. You must also make it a point to learn to hone your skills. You must learn how you can properly manage to control yourself and your emotions while also recognizing the truth of the matter: That you need to ensure that you can recognize your emotions.

Let's look back at the empath for a moment—most empaths struggle with being able to interact with other people for very long. The emotions that they feel tend to become too overwhelming, and they instead choose to not have to engage at all. However, that does not have to be the case. There is no reason that you have to engage as an empath. You can learn to reject those highly volatile emotions so that you can be more in control.

For the empath that is out of control and unable to manage how they feel, or who is constantly feeling overwhelmed, being able to stop and remind yourself of one thing—that you are able to engage with the world from a Stoic perspective, could be the change that you are looking for. Remember, the Stoics do not want to mute your emotions—they just want you to reflect upon them.

Within this chapter, we are going to go over some keys to being able to control yourself. We are going to take a look at how the empath can become Stoic, following those Stoic principles to avoid being entirely overwhelmed whenever emotions start to run high. If you know what you are doing, you can begin to take control; you can learn to be the person that you have always wanted to be. Now, let's take a look at what you can do to control yourself and become a Stoic Empath.

Develop Your Control

We do not control much in life at all. We have gone over this repeatedly. As an empath, you probably know this better than anyone—you cannot control the emotions when they run through you. However, you can control one thing: Your thoughts. We have asserted this. Epictetus was a slave—he was born into slavery and crippled when his master broke his leg. He lived in poverty and died there, too. However, despite the fact that he had no control over his body, he still controlled his thoughts.

Think about this as an empath for a moment—you may not control your feelings, but you can control your thoughts about them. You can remind yourself that you have no reason to get frustrated when you can take control of how you think. Through controlling your thoughts, you can change your reactions. Instead of getting stressed by emotions, you can remind yourself that ultimately, they are what they are, but they are not your feelings and therefore are none of your concern, so you should move on. When you can recognize that you can control your mind and thoughts, you will become much happier than you thought you could be.

Protect Your Time

We oftentimes are loose with our time. We waste it scrolling through social media or not doing anything important. However, unlike literally everything else in life, which we can get more of, time can never be reclaimed. You can make more money. You can buy more things. You can even make more children or remarry a new spouse. However, nothing that you do will ever turn back time.

Remember this. Protect your time from everyone around you. In particular, you must guard that time alone to recharge so that you know that you are able to properly cope with everything that you face in your life. If you want to be comfortable with yourself, you need to be able to control the way that you think or feel. If you want to live a life of happiness, you must be able to protect the time for yourself.

Recognize Happiness Is From Within

Remember that while you may act in ways that you do because you want to be accepted by those around you, true happiness is found within yourself. It does not come from external sources, such as how you engage with someone else or what you can do for them. True happiness is not dependent upon how other people choose to interact with you.

As an empath, it can be easy to give in to hope that other people will be happier with you or will like you more when you do so. However, you are under no obligation to give to other people to make them happy—in fact; you should avoid doing exactly that. Make sure that you only work for internal happiness. Find that true Eudaimonia—that inner joy. It does not have to be outsourced. Other people are not responsible for making you happy, just like you are not responsible for their happiness.

Keep Your Focus

As an empath, it is easy to get distracted all around you with all of the noises and emotional pollution in the air. It is incredibly easy to get distracted in the moment, to give up trying to do something a certain way if you do not know what you are doing. It can be easy to get entirely sidetracked, to feel like if you do not do something a certain way, there will be a problem.

However, remind yourself that you can choose. You can learn to pick and choose what matters the most to you. You can figure out what it is that you want to do so that you can be successful. If you want to be able to guarantee that your interactions with other people are not constantly being sidetracked, you need to learn how you can focus.

Stoics emphasizes that we must make it a point to act, not by reaction, but by purposeful action. Make sure that you focus on what you want to do and keep your mind on it. Mindfully focus. Let yourself stay entirely dedicated to what matters in that moment. If you can do so, you will be far more successful than you imagined.

Get Rid of Ego

We regularly find ourselves caught up in believing that ultimately, we are the most important aspects of our lives. We get stuck in this belief that we are what matters the most—and sure, in our own lives, we are the center. However, it is important to recognize that we are not all-important. This is a lesson that empaths, in particular, need to learn. While you may be quick to shrug this one off and say that you are not egotistical, when is the last time that you assumed that you were the root of a problem rather than it being entirely unrelated to you? Have you told yourself that when someone close to you was upset that it was your own fault? That is egotistical.

Remember, you do not know everything. You are not omnipotent. You do not know what is going on in someone else's mind. Let go of the idea that you are more important than you are and remind yourself of the insignificance of each and every one of us. The universe is constantly growing and changing. Things varied greatly now form a year ago. This is normal. However, what is not normal is believing that you are at the heart of it all. Let go of that belief. Move on. Even if you feel bad about something, it is probably not on you.

Write Often

Journaling is powerful for just about anyone—so powerful that we have seen it repeatedly throughout the book. Make sure that you take the time every day to journal. It is good for you. Reflect on the day that you had. Take the time to consider the way in which you responded to someone or something. Remember the truth of the matter—that you can change your own interactions with ease if you know what you are doing. You just have to reflect and learn.

Be Firm

Remember that you should be firm with yourself. Do not back down. Stand your ground. No matter what it is that someone requests of you, remind yourself that you ought to be true to your virtues. Do not forget that ultimately, you owe yourself one thing: Being true to yourself.

It can be difficult in this day and age—especially if you are a woman, you have probably been taught repeatedly that you owe people your help or that you must make yourself likable. However, that is not the case. You owe nothing. You should remember to be firm and true to your values so that you can be successful in your life. Do not let other people drag you down. Do not let the way that other people see you change how you behave. Always do what is right for you without regard to other people—it will help you immensely.

If you know that something is right, stand firm. It will help you avoid letting other people take advantage of you.

Imagine the Worst Case Scenario

While we have talked about how anxiety is a problem, being able to stop and consider the negativity or worst case scenario, without letting it hold you back, is a practice in temperance. Remember, you must be able to overcome your fear—that means that fear must be present to some degree.

Inviting that contemplation into what may eventually be the case is a great way for you to stop and consider those fears so that you can learn from them. Take some time to think about what might happen if things go wrong. Then, consider how you can handle those situations and how you can or should change what you do today in anticipation.

Ask yourself what things would look like if things went wrong tomorrow or next week.

Ask yourself how you would cope with that particular situation if it were to arise.

Ask yourself if you need to change your life today to cope with tomorrow.

The truth is, you do not have to change today for tomorrow, and even if things go wrong tomorrow, could you really have changed them in the first place? This teaches you resilience and tolerance—both of which matter immensely.

Accept That Nothing Lasts Forever

Finally, remind yourself that nothing in life is forever. Everything will die at some point. The sun will stop shining. The earth will disappear. This is only natural—things age, decay, and die. And ultimately, nothing that you do today will change that. Nothing that you do can prevent that ultimate ending, which means that you need to think accordingly. You need to plan accordingly. You must make sure that what you do in life will bring you joy today. This means that you do not have to let yourself be used by other people—in the grand scheme of things, it is worthless and futile to even bother. You do not have to chase accomplishments hoping to do something grand—no one will remember it. Live your life on your own terms. Live a life that you enjoy. That is the only way to live a good, true life, according to the Stoics, and that is entirely applicable to the empath as well.

Conclusion

Thank you for making it through to the end of *Stoicism & Empathy.* Hopefully, you found this book and everything within it to be highly beneficial to you as you read it! As you read, you were introduced to a wide range of topics designed to benefit you. From being able to recognize the truth all around you to be able to see how empaths can absorb too much emotions and how to prevent it, this book was meant to provide you with information that you could use to live your best life out in a world where nothing lasts forever. You deserve to live a life that you can enjoy, no matter what kind of life that is.

Remember, ultimately, being able to live stoically is highly beneficial to the empath. Being a Stoic empath is just one way that you can make sure that you defend yourself and your mind from the anxiety and stress that can come with the constant inundation of emotions that are common. With the Stoic mindset, you can remind yourself what really matters. You can learn to live a life led by logic and reason instead of constantly being exposed to your emotions. All you have to do is take the time to apply it.

The next step for you is to get started Start using some of those tools that were provided so that you can successfully change the way that you treat those around you. Make sure that you are constantly working to better yourself and the control that you have over yourself so that you are able to succeed in minding your emotions and living a successful life. It does not take much to begin living life Stoically, and the benefits that it can bring can be life-changing if you can learn how to utilize them accordingly.

Thank you for taking the time to reach the end of this book. As you read, hopefully, you learned something new that you can begin to apply to your own life! Hopefully, you are feeling more empowered now than ever, and like you can take back the control over your life once and for all. Good luck as you dive deeper into these different states of mind so that you can begin to live the life that you want to lead. Thank you once more, and please, if you found that this book was beneficial to you in any way or helped you out, head over to Amazon to leave a quick review! Support from the readers is always greatly appreciated and highly recommended!

Printed in Great Britain
by Amazon